T0162799

Other Books by Dr. Samuel White, III

Loving the Soul: How to Love

Healing Your Soul: Christian Self-Care

Hope for Your Soul: Words of Encouragement

Caring for Your Soul: Improving Your Life

Sex and the Soul: Overcoming Temptation

Dying in Peace: Preparing for Eternity

Aging Gracefully: Spiritual Care for Aging Adults

*My Brothers Keeper: Church Ministry for
Young African American Males*

No More Tears: Comfort for the Grieving

The Capitalist Christian Contradiction: God Against Greed

All books are available at Westbow Press and other online

IT IS WELL
with
MY SOUL

Spiritual Care for the Dying

DR. SAMUEL WHITE III

WESTBOW
PRESS®
A DIVISION OF THOMAS NELSON
& ZONDERVAN

Scripture taken from the King James Version of the Bible.

WestBow Press books may be ordered through booksellers or by contacting:

WestBow Press
A Division of Thomas Nelson & Zondervan
1663 Liberty Drive
Bloomington, IN 47403
www.westbowpress.com
1 (866) 928-1240

ISBN: 978-1-4908-3010-0 (e)
ISBN: 978-1-4908-2333-1 (sc)

Library of Congress Control Number: 2014901154

Print information available on the last page.

Printed in the United States of America.

WestBow Press rev. date: 04/01/2019

CONTENTS

ACKNOWLEDGMENTS

Thanks to our Lord and Savior, Jesus Christ who saved my soul.

Thanks to my wife, Sandra, daughter, Alexandria, and son, Samuel IV, who love my soul.

Thanks to my parents Samuel, Anna and siblings, David, Dee Ann, Cherise, and Renee' and Van who shaped my soul.

Thanks to all the members of Friendship Baptist Church and all my co-workers of Hospices of Henry Ford, who inspire my soul.

Thanks to all hospice patients and their families who taught my soul.

It is because of all of you that I can proclaim, "It is Well with my Soul."

PREFACE

One of the most heart-wrenching experiences of my life was watching my father deteriorate and die from cancer. I had never seen such a horrifying metamorphosis in my life. The cancer and chemotherapy had grossly disfigured his forty-nine-year-old frame. His strong, robust body had become skeletal, weak, fragile, and listless. His skin became ashen, his eyes were glossy, and his breathing was labored. My father was dying of cancer, and my soul was dying of sorrow.

My mother and I sat speechless in the hospital room. I held his thin, frail hand, and my mother sat beside his bed. His hands were sweaty and could barely grasp mine. I did not know what to say to him or what to do. All my seminary training at Harvard Divinity School and fifteen years of pastoral experience had not prepared me for this. It seemed as if we were waiting for an eternity. I felt empty, broken, and useless. I did not have the words or the skills to cope with the kaleidoscope of feelings I had, let alone theirs.

What could I say to my father to encourage his faith and strengthen his soul? What words could I use to comfort my mother's broken heart? I was furious that God was allowing my Father to die such a tortuous death at a young age. It was hard for me to believe in a good and merciful God when my father was dying such a cruel and painful death. Our souls were restless with grief, anger, doubt and despair.

My grieving mother sat by his bed and watched my father take deep, long labored breaths. She was beyond tears, beyond words, full of despair and bewildered by it all. Her silent tears broke my heart. We both sat in silence. We heard nothing but my father's death rattle.

Then I remembered the last thing my father told me, "If I live, praise God and if I die, praise God, either way, I am blessed." As we talked about my fathers' final words, we felt encouraged. The remembrance and retelling of his powerful words resurrected our hearts and souls. The fact that my father was at peace enabled my mother and I to have peace, we could now begin to accept my father's impending death knowing that he was in Gods' hands.

My fathers' testimony reminded me of Horatio Spafford's popular hymn, "It is well with my soul." Horatio Spafford tragically lost his children in a shipwreck and in his grief penned these immortal words, "When peace like a river attendeth my way. When sorrows like sea billows roll. Whatever my lot thou hast taught me to say it is well. It is well with my soul." It is well with my soul are words of one who has accepted death and found meaning in it. They have chosen a triumphant attitude in the face of devastation and loss. "It is well with my soul" can only be said by those whose soul is filled with the grace and peace of God and have come to a place in their life when they are at peace with God, others, themselves and their circumstances.

This is the kind of inner tranquility that we all seek, especially when we are close to dying. As a pastor and hospice chaplain, church members, hospice patients, and their families have asked me for a scripture, positive thought, or meditation that would meet their spiritual wounds and give them a sense of peace. They yearned for a word of comfort that would adequately address their erratic emotional needs and faltering faith.

If there is ever a time when the soul needs to be healed, it is during the death and dying process. Unaddressed issues about one's faith, family, focus, faults, finances, feelings, and the finite can create an existential crisis. Often, spiritual sickness will go undiagnosed or unrecognized. Consequently, many of the dying are unprepared for death, and their caregivers are ill equipped to serve them. Despite the pioneering work of Elizabeth Kubler Ross and others there is still not enough information on how to give spiritual care to the dying, and too many questions remain unanswered.

What do you say to someone who is getting ready to die? How can you provide spiritual support to someone whose life is ending? What words do you use to soothe a dying person hurting heart and ease their troubled mind? How can the dying find meaning in life and draw closer to God? How does one prepare a dying persons soul for death? What spiritual assessment can a pastor, hospice clinician, chaplain, clergy, social worker, nurse, grief counselor, or caregiver use to discover the spiritual exigencies of the dying and prepare them for death? How does one deal with spiritual sickness and pain? What spiritual interventions can one use to provide good spiritual care? What can one do to provide spiritual healing for the dying?

It is well with my soul: Spiritual Care for the Dying will answer some of these spiritual inquiries. It is my hope this work will be a spiritual resource for pastors, hospice clinicians, chaplains, nurses, health aides, grief counselors, social workers, and caregivers as they prepare people for death. Hopefully, the insights offered in this work will enlighten those who care for the terminally ill and consequently the dying will be able to say in their own words, "It is well with my soul."

Chapter 1 is a *Spiritual Assessment* that will assist those who care for the dying and help them to determine the healthiness of a terminally ill person's soul. Questions about a person's faith, family, feelings, focus, failures, finances, and the finite will enable pastors, hospice clinicians, clergy, social workers, grief counselors, and caregivers discover the needs of the dying persons' soul.

Chapter 2 speaks to *Spiritual Sickness* contracted by some of the dying. Spiritual sickness of the soul has its expressions in meaninglessness, fear, sadness/despair, alienation/loneliness, and guilt. Each of these spiritual sicknesses has symptoms and spiritual interventions that can lead to spiritual healing. Also, we will discuss the symptoms of Alzheimer's and Dementia patients and how to render spiritual care.

Chapter 3's subject is *Spiritual Care*, it tells how pastors, nurses, social workers, hospice clinicians, clergy, health aides and caregivers can provide spiritual care for the dying. Spiritual interventions like logo therapy, life review, loving, listening and learning prepare the dying for death and can lead to inner serenity.

Chapter 4 is a resource of *Spiritual Meditations* that pastors, nurses, social worker, hospice clinicians, health aides, grief counselors and caregivers can read to the terminally ill. These spiritual meditations deal with a wide variety of issues and feelings. Each meditation is followed by a brief prayer and reflective questions that can deepen spiritual understanding. These meditations can be a source of comfort and strength.

Chapter 5 offers *Spiritual Care Plans* that the chaplain, social worker, nurse, grief counselor and the hospice clinician can use as they care for the dying. Spiritual care plan is driven by the dying patients concerns, has measurable goals and reveals the outcome of the services rendered.

Chapter 6 shares how *Spiritual Healing* can occur when the needs of the soul are addressed through the reading, hearing and believing in the Holy Scriptures. An index of scriptures has been compiled for the clergy, nurse, social worker, hospice clinician or caregivers use. When Biblical therapy is given to the dying it can give them inner peace and comfort.

One of the worse things that could befall a person is to die with the needs of their soul undiagnosed and unattended. Terminal restlessness, existential frustration and despair experienced by many dying people is due to the neglect or unawareness of the soul's sickness. We must properly diagnose the soul's diseases and provide the appropriate spiritual interventions to bring spiritual healing and peace to the dying.

All of the characters and illustrations were fictionalized to exemplify the spiritual necessities of the dying and various ways to address them. The imaginary stories presented in this book provide spiritual insight and practical information.

It is Well with My Soul is for anyone who wants to learn how to be an effective spiritual care provider and assist their loved ones with a peaceful transition into the next life. Giving comfort to our dying loved ones is the most precious and greatest gift we can give them. The last days and hours that we spend with them are extremely valuable and critical to the peacefulness of their souls. I hope that *It is well with my soul* will be a source of peace for those who are going thru this journey.

CHAPTER

1

SPIRITUAL ASSESSMENT

A spiritual assessment is critical to the vitality and wellbeing of the soul. It is especially important during the death and dying process that the pastor, hospice clinician, clergy, nurse, social worker, health aide or caregiver ask the dying some deeply revealing and provocative questions. It is imperative that we determine whether the dying persons' soul is healthy and prepared for death. It is the neglect, refusal, or ignorance of the needs of the soul that fosters spiritual sickness. A spiritual assessment is needed to discover the maladies of the soul. It is important to know what unresolved negative feelings, issues, behaviors, thoughts, and concerns the terminally ill are struggling with. Socrates is right, "The unexamined life is a life not worth living." A spiritual assessment that examines the needs and sicknesses of the soul is a prerequisite to providing good spiritual care and spiritual well-being. A pastor, hospice clinician, clergy, nurse, social worker, home health aide or caregiver can use this spiritual assessment to discover the dying person's spiritual exigencies. This assessment can be broken into seven spiritual concerns: family, feeling, faith, focus, faults, finances, and finite being. Inquiries in these seven spiritual concerns will enlighten the spiritual care provider on the needs of the dying person's soul.

Seven Spiritual Concerns

I. Family

One of the major concerns terminally ill people have is reconciliation with their families. The family is a social group or construct of individuals who may or may not be related to the dying person. It is the group of relationships that shape the soul and release it into life. The soul is shaped by dysfunctional relationships, healthy relationships, family secrets, broken relationships, adversarial relationships, mentoring relationships, heartbreaks, and heart healings. When we talk about family, we are not just referring to blood relatives. I define family as those who are intimately involved with the dying and had some impact on his or her heart, mind, or soul. The following questions about a terminally ill person's family will enable a pastor, hospice chaplain, clergy, clinician, or caregiver to discover who the terminally ill person's family is and what kind of impact they have on them.

1. Who helped to raise you, and how do you feel about them?
2. Who do you consider family, and how did they influence you?
3. When is the last time you told your family you loved them?
4. What kind of relationships do you have with your family?
5. Have you ever been abused, neglected, or rejected by family members? Who and why?
6. Have you ever talked to the family member about your personal issues, and what was their response?
7. Is there something you need to forgive a family member?
8. Are there any unresolved family issues that need to be dealt with?
9. Are you willing to express unconditional love to have peace?
10. Is there anything you need to say or do with a family member?
11. What do you need to hear from your family members and why?

12. Do you need any family member to show you his or her love to you?
13. What do you want your family to remember about you?
14. What final message do you want to leave to your family?

Asking questions about dying persons' family will enlighten them about unresolved relational issues. They may need to talk about how they or a loved one was abused and the emotional scars they still have. They may want to apologize and reconcile with someone, on the other hand, they may need to confront a family member and address an issue. The dying person and his or her family may need to express their love to one another. Some dying people have never really discovered who their parents or siblings are. It may be time for the family to come together before it is too late. Terminally ill people's relationships can deeply affect their souls. Broken relationships can break the spirit and wound the soul. Therefore, it requires the pastor, hospice chaplain, clergy member, or caregiver to help the dying to explore all the dynamics of their relationships and if possible, bring about resolution. The goal is for the dying person to be at peace with his relationships. This peace may not mean harmony with a family member, it may mean for the dying person to forgive someone who has not asked for forgiveness, or it may mean acceptance of an unacceptable relationship. The soul can have peace in relationships when it practices unconditional love and acceptance.

II. Feelings

The death and dying process will bring about a kaleidoscope of feelings. There may be times when they feel fear, guilt, loss of control, anger, loneliness and despair, confusion, sadness, frustration, hope, acceptance, and meaninglessness. It is imperative that the pastor, hospice chaplain, clergy person, or caregiver know how the dying person is feeling. The following questions can be asked to discover the terminally ill person's feelings.

1. How do you feel about dying?
2. What are you afraid and anxious about?
3. Is there something that makes you feel agitated and frustrated?
4. Are you afraid of the judgment of God?
5. Do you have concerns about losing your life?
6. Do you have impossible expectations?
7. Are you extra-critical of things, people, and situations?
8. Are you upset because you have limited options?
9. Are you having a difficult time with the fact that death is imminent?
10. Do you feel victimized by life or events?
11. What are you worried about?
12. Do you find it difficult to trust anyone? Why?
13. Do you feel like giving up?
14. Do you feel lonely, empty, or alienated from others?
15. Do you feel as if no one really cares?
16. What do you feel guilty about?
17. Do you feel as if you deserve this illness?
18. Do you feel as if you do not deserve the care you are receiving?
19. What do you regret?
20. Do you feel as if you deserve this illness?
21. Do you feel as if you do not deserve the care you are receiving?
22. Do you reject the people who love and care about you?
23. What are you most sad about?
24. What are you confused about?
25. What makes you frustrated or upset?
26. Are you struggling with meaning in life and death?
27. What is your sense of meaning and purpose in life?
28. What could you do to make the rest of your life meaningful?
29. What unfinished business do you need to do before death?
30. Do you displace your anger? How?
31. Is there anything you wish you could undo, redo, or relive in the past?
32. Do you have an inability to express your feelings?

33. Are you upset or angry with the health care you or your loved one is receiving?
34. Have you accepted the fact that you or your loved one will die?
35. Do you ever feel so hopeless that you want to die?
36. Are you angry or frustrated with God?
37. Is your life joyful?
38. Do you feel restless?

Acknowledging the feelings of the dying is healing. It validates the passion of the person's soul and affirms his or her struggle. There is nothing wrong with feelings. All people have the right to express themselves in their own way. All people have their own unique way of sharing how they feel. A dying person may want to wallow in self-pity or hurl nasty diatribes at God. Some may want to curse you out, others may be angry at the very people who are helping them, and some will be full of worry and anxiety. They may be afraid to die and fearful of losing their loved ones. Whatever they are feeling is their own business. The spiritual care provider has no right to change the way a person may feel. It is their responsibility to help the dying explore their feelings and what they may mean as they relate to their soul. The goal is to validate the terminally ill person's feelings and encourage him or her to discover peace that comes with expressing him or herself.

III. Faith

The faith of terminally ill people is critical to the health of their souls. Faith is not religious dogma or belief. Faith is what one puts one's ultimate trust in. Some people place their faith in God, religion, activity, a philosophy, themselves, or others. Everyone believes in someone or something. The question is, how does the person's faith enable him or her to cope with death and dying? These are just some of the questions that one may ask to determine a person's faith.

1. Do you consider yourself religious, spiritual, or both? Explain.
2. Is your faith a source of comfort or challenge for you? Why?
3. Do you see illness as punishment from God? Why?
4. Is there anything about your religion that you do not know?
5. How has your religion hurt or helped you in coping with death and dying?
6. If God were sitting in front of you, what would you say?
7. What do you think God will say to you on the Day of Judgment and why?
8. Are you angry at religious representatives? Why?
9. What do you want to tell God?
10. What are some of the things you could do to get closer to God?
11. How has your pain and suffering developed or hindered your faith?
12. What do you question God about?
13. Do you believe in life after death? Why or why not?
14. Do you believe in heaven or hell? Why or why not?
15. Why do you believe what you believe in?
16. What are the ways in which you can practice your religion?
17. Do you feel you need to improve yourself? If so, why and in what ways?
18. What does it mean to be saved or born-again, and why do you believe this? Who is God to you?
19. Who is Jesus Christ to you?
20. Do you think God loves you? Why or why not?
21. What could you do to increase your faith?
22. What scriptures or religious writings to you need to hear to strengthen your soul?
23. What parts of your faith need to change?
24. Is your faith too controlling and not accepting?
25. What is your religion?
26. How often do you attend religious services?
27. How much is religion and/or God a source of strength and comfort to you?

28. Do you consider yourself religious?

29. What or who do you have faith in?

Discovering the faith of a terminally ill person will enable the spiritual care provider to lead him or her into spiritual peace. Again, dying people may place their faith in God or in anyone or anything else. Faith is not just a religious doctrine. It is a spiritual word that reveals what one puts one's ultimate trust in. The terminally ill may place their trust in their doctor, their spouse, their religion, or even themselves. The question is not what or who do they place their faith in, but does their faith strengthen or weaken them? Does their faith in their religion, person, or object give them peace or trouble them? Does their faith work for them or against them? The end-of-life experience places demands on one's faith. It may make one reform, reject, or change one's faith. The goal of the pastor, hospice clinician, clergy, or caregiver is helping the dying reflect on their faith and change or strengthen it so they may have a sense of peace.

Four Types of Faith

There are four types of faith that terminally ill people may have during the dying process, conventional faith, controlling faith, crushed faith, or consolidated faith. Conventional faith gives a sense of order and meaning in people's lives. It is a faith in the basic principles of the protestant religion. Those who have a Conventional faith believe in God, the Bible, the Christian Church, Heaven and Hell, the Holy Spirit, and the death, burial and resurrection of Jesus Christ. The negative aspect of this kind of faith is that it struggles with undeserved pain and suffering. Those dying person with Conventional Faith asks questions like, "Why isn't God answering my prayers? Why is this happening to me? Where is God, and when will He deliver me?"

Controlling faith gives a sense of hope and security during overwhelming circumstances. The downside of controlling faith is that it is rigid, and cannot accept pain, sickness, and suffering. Terminally ill persons with controlling faith never stop believing that God will heal them and grant them a miracle. They find it extremely difficult to accept the fact that they are dying, they get frustrated that God has not yet taken them to glory and wonder what is taking God so long. They want to control the uncontrollable. People with Controlling Faith can become disillusioned and upset that they cannot control their God, family, wellbeing, and life. Often dying people with a Controlling Faith end up with Crushed Faith and express it with anger, hopelessness, and despair. They may be angry and frustrated that God has not answered their prayers in their own way and time frame.

People with Crushed Faith may stop believing in God, religion, church, and all expressions of faith. They have lost hope and have resigned themselves to a life of despair. They doubt everything and everybody, and often they feel lonely, isolated, and detached from friends, family, and all those who support them. The biblical character Job, who lost his health and wealth, revealed Crushed Faith when he said, "Let the day perish wherein I was born...." (Job 3:3)

Interestingly, as Job expressed his doubt and despair to his friends and God, he developed a Consolidated Faith, the other side of Crushed Faith which integrates undeserved suffering and spiritual strength. Terminally persons who have Consolidated Faith have embraced the fact that they are dying and have found meaning in it. They still believe in God despite unanswered prayers, long suffering, and bouts of disbelief. This is the ultimate development of faith because it does not seek to control, it has no illusions, and it is not grounded in a religious dogma or a "Pollyanna" perspective.

There is no one who better expresses a Consolidated Faith than our Lord and Savior Jesus Christ. In the garden of Gethsemane, Jesus prayed that the cup of suffering would pass Him. Jesus did not want to suffer and die. He did not want to be crucified and die a painful death. Jesus struggled with accepting His death until He concluded His prayer with the powerful words, "Thy will be done."(Matthew 26:42) Once Jesus said, "Thy will be done," He was able to endure the humiliating, degrading treatment of the Sanhedrin and the cruelty and brutality of the Roman soldiers. Once Jesus said, "Thy will be done." He was at peace within Himself, with God, and with death. The only way for a dying person to have this kind of inner serenity is to be able to say, "Thy will be done." It is only in accepting the unacceptable and bearing the unbearable that we discover the peace of God. The Serenity Prayer expresses this kind of peace and Consolidated Faith: "God grant me the serenity to accept the things I cannot change, the courage to change the things I can, and the wisdom to know the difference."

1. Conventional Faith

This is a traditional belief system that believes in a Supreme Being, a sense of right and wrong, and spiritual meritocracy. People with this kind of faith have a difficult time accepting undeserved suffering and premature death. They may express doubts, frustration, and anger. The pastor, hospice clinician or caregiver should validate dying people's feelings and help them to reflect, reassess and redevelop their faith.

2. Controlling Faith

People with controlling faith have a rigid, uncompromising belief system that believes a supreme being will heal them and sickness is an aberration of their faith. Some believe sickness means there is a lack of faith in God's ability to heal. They believe that if they just keep on praying, somehow, some way they will receive a miracle. It never occurs to them that death can be considered a form of deliverance and a miracle. Those with Controlling Faith inevitably become angry, disillusioned, and bitter. The pastor, hospice clinician, caregiver, and clergy person will validate the feelings of those with controlling faith and help them to reflect on what Dr. Weatherby called the "unintentional will of God." The spiritual care provider will educate the dying on the meaning of faith as it surrenders its control to God.

3. Crushed Faith

Terminally ill people with Crushed Faith are going through a faith crisis in which they have serious doubts about God and their entire belief system. Their sickness and terminality make them question everything. Some may share their feelings of hopelessness and despair. They are alienated from others and God. Like our Lord suffering on the cross, they may utter, "My God, my God, why hast thou forsaken me?" (Matthew 27:46) Those who are caring for the dying must be willing to listen to all their bitterness and hopelessness without judging them. A loving presence and a listening ear will do wonders for those who are experiencing a Crushed Faith.

4. Consolidated Faith

Dying people with Consolidated Faith may believe in a supreme being and have yielded to the will of God in their lives. They have accepted the fact that they will die. Their faith doesn't reject or ignore sickness. It accepts and finds meaning in it. They may see their suffering as a stimulus for their spiritual growth and as an opportunity to witness to others about the grace of God in their lives. Those with Consolidated Faith may share their hopes of a life beyond this life. They are blessed with an inner peace and are spiritually prepared to meet their Maker. A pastor, hospice clinician or caregiver may validate these people's feelings and faith.

Assessing a Patient's Faith

The pastor, hospice clinician, grief counselor, or caregiver can determine the kind of faith the dying person has by asking some poignant questions. Some questions one may want to ask are: How is your faith or belief? Is your faith strong, steady, or weak? Do you believe you are getting better or worse? How do you feel about dying? What gives you spiritual strength? Another way of determining the faith is by listening intently to the person's spiritual story, feelings, beliefs, or goals. Sometimes the dying person will share a prayer request indicating his or her faith perspective.

Or dying people's feelings may indicate their belief systems. If they are expressing hopelessness and despair, they may have a Crushed Faith. If they are still talking unrealistically about miracles, they may have a Controlling faith. If they are struggling with their faith and are unsure of what to believe, they may have a Conventional Faith. The spiritual goal is that the dying may obtain a Consolidated Faith and be at peace within themselves, with the dying process, with others, and with God.

IV. Focus

The dying person may focus on a variety of things. Focus is what your short-term and long-term interests are. A short-term focus could be pain medication, the next meal, getting another blanket, and waiting for a nurse or family member. Whatever their immediate interest becomes their focus. The long-term focus represents their goals in life. Or it could be their primary interest or passion in life. For some people, their passions are hobbies, sports, gardening, a job, fishing, family, music, or missions. Whatever brings them overwhelming joy and peace is their focus. Therefore, fulfilling their focus should strengthen their soul. What becomes problematic for dying people is that often they must change the long-term focus of their lives. The following questions will enlighten the clergy, social worker, nurse, health aide or caregiver about the focus or passion of the terminally ill person's life.

1. What is the primary focus in your life? What do you need right now?
2. What are the things you do that bring peace and pleasure?
3. What are your hobbies, and how could you practice them?
4. What is it that you take great interest in?
5. When you die, what will be your legacy?
6. What are the things you enjoy doing?
7. What gives you peace of mind?
8. What puts a smile on your face and joy in your heart?
9. What could you do to make your life meaningful?
10. Are you ready to meet your Maker?
11. What do you want to accomplish in this life?
12. What goals have you been able to achieve in life?
13. What are you able to still do?
14. What are your immediate concerns?
15. What could you do to address your immediate needs?
16. What can you do with the time you have left?
17. Does life seem empty?
18. Is your life joyful?

It is vitally important that the nurse, social worker, health aide, clergy, or caregiver discover and address the immediate needs of the dying. If it is water give, them something to drink. If they are hungry, feed them. If they are cold, give them a blanket. If they are bored, read a book, listen to music, or watch TV with them. Spiritual care means to respond to the immediate needs of the terminally ill.

The long-range focus or passions of the dying must be discovered, supported, or changed if they are to experience peace. The spiritual care provider must find creative ways for the dying to fulfill their passions. There was a hospice patient who was confined to her nursing home room and was unable to go outside. The major problem was that she loved to be outside because she was an avid gardener. She had a big, beautiful garden at home. She longed to go back home and see her flowers. I asked her daughter to take pictures of her mother's garden, put them in a picture album, and give it to her. When the daughter gave it to her mother, she shed tears. She was so happy to look at the pictures of her garden. She beamed with pride and joy. She loved looking at her garden. She was not able to attend it, but she still could appreciate it and dream about it. For this woman, to be reconnected to her passion brought her peace. Spiritual care means to help the dying find creative ways to fulfill their passion and experience peace.

V. Faults

Some terminally ill persons will want to deal with their own personal sins and shortcomings. They may want to examine some of their faults and failures as they prepare themselves to meet their Maker. Their sense of guilt and shame maybe robbing them of peace of mind, or their past transgressions may have ruptured their relationships with their loved ones, and they yearn to make amends. The spiritual care provider can help them to reflect on their bad behaviors, habits, decisions, and lifestyle that may impact the healthiness of the soul. The following questions can be used to help the dying discover areas of their lives that they may want to deal with.

1. Is there anything you have done in the past that you are ashamed of and need to confess?
2. Is there anyone you have hurt to whom you need to apologize?
3. Do you have any bad habits you need to deal with?
4. Are you an alcoholic or substance abuser?
5. Do you have an addictive personality that enslaves you to persons, property, prosperity, or passions?
6. Is there anything or anyone you love more than God?

7. Are you in control of your passions, or are your passions in control of you?
8. What are your bad habits?
9. What are your vices or weaknesses?
10. Do you have any secret sins or skeletons in the closet?
11. Are you pleased with your relationship with God?
12. What do you think God will say to you on the Day of Judgment?
13. What could you do to improve yourself?
14. Are there any sexual sins, behaviors, relationships, or passions you need to repent of?
15. Have you been freed from your sins?
16. Do you feel as if God has forgiven you of your sins?
17. Do you consider yourself a moral or ethical person? Why or why not?
18. What do you feel guilty about?
19. What are you ashamed of?
20. Have you prayed to God and asked God to forgive you of your faults and failures?

Coming to grips with one's shortcomings is not an easy thing to do. Oftentimes people avoid asking themselves difficult questions. Or they reject or ignore persons who dare to ask them about their faults. Many people do not want to be reminded of the transgressions of their souls, however impending death can motivate people to take a good, hard look at themselves. Some feel the time they have left should be used to prepare themselves for the judgment of God. Others are so overwhelmed with guilt and shame that they feel a need to confess to someone or something. The spiritual care provider can help a dying person become aware of their faults and if possible, deal with them.

A fifty-three-year old hospice patient with a history of alcoholism wanted to be reconciled with his adult children, who he had not seen in ten years. He had expressed a lot of guilt and remorse that he had verbally abused and ignored them. He really did not think they wanted to see him. As his hospice chaplain, I helped him to forgive himself and seek out the forgiveness of his children. I spoke to his family several times and encouraged them to reconcile with their father before it was too late. Fortunately, they did meet with their dying father, and they were able to forgive one another. This would not have been possible if the dying father did not want to deal with his faults.

VI. Finances

Terminally ill people may have financial or material concerns as they live out their last days. Financial concerns are not just monetary but encompass one's entire material wellbeing. Some dying persons maybe concerned with sky-rocketing medical costs, outstanding bills, living expenses, funeral arrangements, food, shelter, clothing, wellbeing of family, nursing home problems, will, medical power of attorney, life insurance, selfishness, greed, hoarding, death beneficiaries, and any other material concerns. If some of these material issues are unresolved, the soul may not experience peace. Jesus tells the parable of the rich fool who built bigger barns to warn us of the spiritual dangers of greed and hoarding. In the parable God ask the selfish rich man, "Fool! This night your soul will be required of you; then whose will those things be which you have provided?" (Luke 12:16–20). This is a spiritual question we all must address, especially those who are terminally ill. Getting our financial house in order before we die should be a priority.

A Spiritual Care Provider will need to ask questions of the terminally ill about their financial or material wellbeing. The answer to these inquiries will enable them to discover what areas they will need to work on as they prepare their souls for eternity. Resolving these financial issues will grant the dying inner tranquility. The following questions can be asked to determine the material needs of the dying.

1. Are you concerned about the medical cost related to your health? If so, what are you doing about it?
2. Do you have some outstanding debts you are worried about?
3. Are you able to pay your expenses?
4. Have you made funeral arrangements? If you haven't, when will you?
5. Does someone know where your insurance, will, and other important papers are?
6. Are you satisfied with the food?
7. Are you satisfied with where you live?
8. Are you in need of any clothing or material needs?
9. Are you concerned about the wellbeing of your family?
10. How do you feel about this nursing home?
11. Do you have a will? If not, when will you write one?
12. Have you made your wishes known about whom you want your things to go to?
13. Do you have a medical power of attorney? If not, when will you get one?
14. is your life insurance current, and does someone know where it is?
15. Are you selfish with your property and possessions?
16. You cannot take your worldly treasures with you. Who do you want to give them to, and when will you give them?
17. Are you a greedy person? If you are, why not be more giving?
18. Are you hoarding clothes, shoes, hats, coats, suits, jewelry, property, and possessions? Why not begin to give some of those things to the needy?
19. When you die, who do you want to be your beneficiary? Is it documented someplace, and does someone know about it?
20. Do you have any material, financial, legal, or social concerns?

Asking these questions will disclose the terminally person's pressing financial issues. Some of these issues are so important to dying people that their souls cannot find peace until they are resolved. As a hospice chaplain, I counseled a dying man whose only desire was to leave the nursing home, go back home, and find his insurance papers. Despite this man's physical limitations and weaknesses, he took the bus home and found his documents. For him there was nothing more pressing than finding his insurance papers. Once he found his documents, his soul was at peace.

I have assisted dying person come to grips with harsh realities of living in an impoverished nursing home and learning to accept the cramped quarters, unseasoned food, and inconsistent and sometimes inconsiderate help of nursing home staff. Acceptance and tolerance of unchangeable living arrangements brings about an inner peace. Caregivers may have to assist dying persons in the distribution of their property and possessions. Many families have literally fought over the dying person's possessions, and the dying person could not rest until it was resolved. Some of these questions may open the eyes of the dying person's selfishness and materialism. They may want to begin to give their things away to their family, friends, and those in need. Pastors may encourage the dying to make their funeral arrangements. Quite a few of the members of my church wanted to make sure their funeral service was arranged before they died. The spiritual care provider can be an enormous help getting the terminally ill person's financial house in order.

VII. Finite

One of the most pressing concerns of the terminally is that they are finite, or their existence is limited. Some people will be in denial of their impending death. Others will be fearful and anxious. Some may even be angry at the thought of death. Many will be saddened and depressed. Then there are those few people who have accepted death and have even prepared their own funeral services. How patients cope with their impending death can say a lot about the status of their souls. If they have accepted their terminality and have discovered meaning in it, their souls are strong. If they are struggling with the thought of dying, then their souls are moderately healthy, but, if they are in denial of death or using religion as an opiate, then their souls are weak. A patient whose soul is healthy is at peace with death, with others, with himself, and with God. The following questions can be asked to determine how the patient is coping with his or her impending death:

1. How do you feel about dying?
2. Are you ready to die?
3. Do you believe in God, and if you do, what do you think He will say to you when you die?
4. What do you think will happen to you when you die?
5. Are you afraid of dying? What are you afraid of?
6. Are your loved ones prepared for you to die?
7. What do you need to do to prepare for death?
8. Are you at peace with the way you are dying?
9. Have you found meaning in your death?
10. What lessons or wisdom have you gleaned from your impending death?
11. Are you at peace with others?
12. Are you at peace with yourself? Can you say, "It is well with my soul"? Why or why not?

A spiritual assessment rendered by a spiritual care provider must always be done with sensitivity and patience, understanding that all dying persons have their own spiritual uniqueness and character, moreover, each person may have some concerns that are more pressing than others. Some people will want to deal with a family concern, others may feel the need to address a focus, like getting pain medication. Whatever the terminally ill wants to talk about or needs is what the spiritual care provider should deal with. The dying person sets the agenda, and not the spiritual care provider. They will fulfill the spiritual assessment in their own time frame and in their own way.

The Terminally ill Spiritual Hierarchy of Needs

The most important needs confronting dying patients are those that stem from the soul. Spiritual needs like feeling, focus, faith, finite, family, faults and financial welfare are critical to the welfare of the soul. Contrary to Abraham Maslow's hierarchy of needs, the dying patient's spiritual needs take precedence over their physical needs. The spiritual care provider asks questions to discover the patient's spiritual needs and address them. A level of trust must be developed to move from one level of need to another.

First Level: Question the Patient's Feelings

Patient's level of pain is the first thing that must be addressed.

Second Level: Questions the Patient's Focus

Patient's short- and long-term goals are discovered and developed.

Third Level: Questions the Patient's Faith

Patient is encouraged to discover what kind of faith they have.

Fourth Level: Question the Patient's Finiteness

Patient's finite status is addressed. Patient is asked if he or she is ready to die. Patient is encouraged to accept their terminality and find peace with their Supreme Being.

Fifth Level: Questions the Patient's Family

Patient's faults are delicately disclosed and personally dealt with.

Sixth Level: Questions the Patient's Faults

Patient's faults are delicately addressed. Patient learns to be honest with themselves and with others

Seventh Level: Questions the Patient's Finances

Patient's financial, material or physical welfare is dealt with.

Spiritual Self-Assessment

The Bible admonishes us, "Examine yourselves, whether ye be in the faith, prove your own selves…." II. Corinthians 13:15. The most detrimental thing one could do for oneself is to die without really knowing who you are and whose you are. We all have a responsibility to ourselves to discover our strengths and weaknesses. We should know the sins, sorrows, and struggles of the soul. We should take time to evaluate and reflect on the condition of our soul. This is especially true of those who are at the end of their lives. The dying must not waste time with trivial pursuits that do not impact the welfare of their souls. A spiritual self-assessment will enable the terminally ill to discover what their spiritual weaknesses are and emphasize their need to address them. Those who are caring for the dying can give this assessment to them. Some dying persons may want to do their own spiritual self-assessment. Tell them to answer the following questions as honestly as possible.

Faith

1. How would you characterize your faith: strong, medium, or weak?
2. What can you do to make your faith stronger?
3. Does your faith in your religion or belief give you peace, or do you need to change it?
4. What kind of faith do you need to have peace?

5. What do you need to do to increase your faith in God?

Feeling

1. How do you feel most of the time and why?
2. How do you feel about dying and why?
3. Do you have control over your feelings, or do your feelings control you? Why?
4. What can you do to give yourself peace and joy?
5. Have you asked God to help you with your feelings?

Focus

1. What are your immediate concerns, and what can you do about them?
2. What is it that you enjoy doing, and how can you do it?
3. What passion or hobbies give you peace, and is there a creative way you can do them?
4. What unfinished business, projects, or dreams do you need to complete to give you peace?
5. What do you think God wants you to do with the rest of your life?
6. Faithfulness to God does not necessarily mean successfulness. The Bible records a parable about a man who could prophesy and do wonderful works but was still condemned (Matt. 7:21–27). Are you faithful to God? Are you doing and saying what He wants you to do?

Family

1. Who do you need to forgive and reconcile with?
2. Who do you need to talk to before you die?
3. Have you told your family and friends that you love them?

4. What is the most important thing you could do for your family?

5. Is there anyone you have hurt and need to apologize to?

6. What could you do in your relationships that will give you peace?

7. What do you think God wants you to do for others before you die?

Failure

1. What are your weaknesses, vices, addictions, and sins?

2. Do you have any regrets or remorse about your past?

3. Is there anyone who you can confess your faults to?

4. Are you ashamed about anything you did?

5. Have you confessed or repented to God for your sins and shortcomings? Have you asked God to help you to change?

Finances

1. Do you have any financial or material concerns?

2. When you die, do you know who you want to have your things?

3. When will you write a will?

4. Does someone know where your will, insurance papers, and other important documents are?

5. When will you make funeral arrangements?

6. Are you concerned or worried about your family's wellbeing?

7. When will you begin to give away your things to the needy?

8. In the final judgment, God judges us based on whether we have given to the hungry, sick, thirsty, naked, homeless, and incarcerated (Matt. 25:31–46). What do you think God will say to you? What could you still do or give to those in need?

The value of this spiritual assessment is determined by how honestly a person is willing to answer these questions. Lying to oneself will only lead to spiritual sickness and discontent. Truthful answers will bring about a spiritual awareness of the maladies of the soul and set one free from self-delusion. If this spiritual self-assessment is done with honesty and integrity, it will mean the beginning of inner peace. A humble and contrite person will enable God to forgive, redeem, transform, heal, liberate, and consecrate his or her soul. A healthy soul is not necessarily a sinless, perfect soul, rather, it is a soul that realizes its own imperfections and finds its grace and strength in God.

CHAPTER

2

SPIRITUAL SICKNESS

Spiritual sickness or distress often manifests itself during the death and dying process. Some dying people may experience terminal restlessness or spiritual distress. Their pain maybe under control but they lack inner peace, they consciously or unconsciously wrestle with unresolved spiritual issues such as meaningless, fear, sadness/despair, alienation/loneliness, doubt/distrust, anger and guilt, these feelings and behaviors are natural and become pathological when they overwhelm a person's personality and behavior. It is natural for people to become sad when they have been given the news of their terminal diagnosis, however when sadness spreads, like cancer eating away all the joy and peace in their lives it becomes a sickness. It is human and understandable for a person to become fearful when death is imminent and when fear becomes a sickness when it prevents people from enjoying the rest of their life. This chapter will explore these six spiritual sicknesses and their symptoms. Moreover, there are specific spiritual interventions for the pastor, hospice clinicians, clergy person, or caregiver to implement. The goal is that the hospice patient be healed of his or her spiritual malady and experience inner peace.

Spiritual Sickness: Meaninglessness

The death and dying process can bring about a sense of emptiness and meaninglessness. It is what Victor Frankel called "an existential vacuum." Spiritual meaninglessness is a distress or illness that can occur when the terminally ill person has a feeling of despair and has no reason to live or die. It's when the soul has lost its *focus*.

Need

Create an awareness of or atmosphere in which interpersonal or intra-psychic pain can be addressed/explored. Assist the terminally ill person to develop a purpose and meaning to live.

Symptoms

- struggling with meaning in life and death
- disturbance in concepts or perception of God or belief systems
- moderate to severe anxiety
- sense of meaninglessness, purposelessness, cynicism
- disrupted spiritual trust leading to doubts about superior being/God
- frantic seeking of advice or support for decisions
- questions credibility of God or belief system
- refusal to communicate with loved ones
- avoidance of or preoccupation with subject of death
- illness seen as punishment from God
- fear of ability to endure suffering
- unresolved feelings about death
- depression, preoccupation, withdrawal, isolation, or hopelessness
- inability to participate in usual religious practices
- disturbance in sleep/rest pattern
- psychosomatic manifestations or pain, not physical

- wish to undo, redo, relive the past
- concern about life after death
- disturbing dreams
- displaces anger toward religious representative
- self-focus or self-destructive behavior (i.e., self-pity, irritability, restlessness)
- inability to forgive self or receive forgiveness
- projection of blame
- bitterness, recrimination
- demanding behavior
- inability to express
- sense of abandonment
- noncompliance with care plan
- seeks spiritual assistance
- sense of sadness and despair

Interventions

- support ways to strengthen and revive past support systems' connections and involvements
- encourage reflection on factors in self-development
- encourage reflection upon relationship of belief system to interpersonal behaviors
- assist in looking at more satisfactory ways of relating to belief system
- when appropriate, refer to professional pastoral counselor
- encourage life review to determine possible issues in development
- encourage reconciliation with past taught belief system
- develop a new meaning and purpose in life

Goals

- reduced symptoms of intra-psychic anguish (i.e., guilt, anxiety, anger, distress)
- meaningful relationship with significant people
- greater consistency between belief system and interpersonal behavior
- increased peace of mind and joy due to pursuit to new goals
- greater involvement in available supportive belief system

Spiritual Sickness: Fear

An emotion of alarm, apprehension, or sense of danger causing one to feel agitated, anxious, powerless, and frightened. The dying fear loss of health, wealth, control, and unknown.

Need

To eliminate feelings of helplessness and anxiety and reinstate calm and sense of wellbeing and trust in self, others, and the transcendent.

Symptoms

- admission of specific fears, fear of the unknown, fear of being alone at the time of death, fear of uncontrolled pain, and fear of the dying process itself
- agitation, restlessness, particularly when alone or at night
- using third-person examples to discuss fears
- history of anxiety disorder and/or panic attacks
- discussion of afterlife, possible retribution for life decisions, sense of unworthiness
- anger toward belief system, caregivers, or self

- specific concerns about the welfare of family and loved ones when patient is no longer here
- sense of disharmony and disconnection and loss of peace

Interventions

- establish trust and rapport and assure patient every effort will be made to keep the patient comfortable and at home with family and loved ones
- listen supportively and non-judgmentally to ascertain fears
- facilitate education of the disease and the dying process
- encourage the expression of fears, and validate fears and concerns
- encourage acceptance of the unknown as a normal part of human experience
- clarify and affirm the patient's/caregiver's understanding of transcendent and afterlife
- create a constructive dialogue about the unresolved fears that will enhance self-value and promote trust in a loving higher power
- use tradition-appropriate sacred texts to explore and clarify possible misconceptions and beliefs
- explore previous coping skills
- use prayer, meditation, poetry, and inward journeying to regain a sense of peace and spiritual wellbeing
- provide assurance of support and assistance to family to work through and resolved grief
- assist in the completion of unfinished tasks and goals

Goals

- eliminate helplessness, fear, and anxiety and establish a sense of peace, wellbeing, and spiritual wholeness by trusting in self, others, and the transcendent

Spiritual Sickness: Sadness/Despair

The loss of control and a sense of instability and insecurity creates an existential despair. The terminally ill have a difficult time with the loss of control in their lives. The threat of death can drastically change their lives. Their whole world has turned upside down, consequently some suffer in frustration and despair at their inability to control their lives. There is an overwhelming sense of sadness and despair.

Need

- finding satisfaction in being able to make choices in spite of circumstances and to have some control over ourselves and life situations

Symptoms

- fear of loss of spirit and becoming only a body; fear of loss of body and becoming only a spirit
- feeling of being victimized by life/events
- sense of injury to integrity of person and can be expressed by outward expression of sadness, anger, loneliness, rage, withdrawal, yearning, unhappiness
- obvious affect expressions (i.e., anger, tense, worried, appearing stressed)
- "losing control over my affairs after I am gone"
- demanding attitude
- denying situation is as bad as it appears
- bewilderment of confusion at changes in bodily performance
- frightened by lack of ability to act or think appropriately (i.e., "What is happening to me?")
- impossible expectations (i.e., "I can still do that," or "Why can't I do that anymore?")

- manipulation to get others to do what the patient wants (i.e., tears, self-pity, anger, inappropriate comments, etc.)
- criticism of how things are done
- anger, which makes the patient feel in control and more powerful
- unwillingness to trust another with decisions/care: "I can do it myself"
- guilt due to inability to meet high expectations
- worry over small details and serious concerns
- regret: "this is beyond my power to remedy"
- dramatizing, making things appear worse/better than they are
- feeling of giving up
- communication of:
- loss of transcendent dimension (life of the spirit)
- loss of routine
- loss of role, diminishing of person's function
- loss of dreams that might have come true

Intervention

- acknowledge person's right to have and express feelings
- helping person to assign meaning to the loss/present situations
- transcendence: helping to locate the person in a large picture
- validate patients feeling of loss of control as real
- respect for patient's positive efforts made
- determine the patient wants to do or take care of despite the illness
- identify realistic goals for illness
- identify realistic goals for illness now
- support patient's efforts that promote his or her own control
- renew life goals already met, as well as regrets of unmet desires

Goals

- affirm personal strengths and recourse (i.e., faith, humor, courage)
- relaxation ideas, music, quietness
- reduce the spiritual suffering, pain
- expression of feeling affirming
- encourage decision-making ability and respect patient's decisions
- acceptance of reality

Spiritual Sickness: Alienation/Loneliness

This is a feeling of being without companions, empty, or without people. Loneliness is a feeling of being alienated, estranged, and separated from others. There can be a disconnect between patient, family, friends, and God. Patients may feel lonely and abandoned

Need

Affirm past and present relationships that will give a renewed spiritual meaning to life.

Symptoms

- lack of meaning
- lack of divine identity
- depression, including crying
- anger and resentment
- lack of visitors and cards
- withdrawn
- rejection of staff, caregivers, and others
- low self-esteem and self-worth

- sense of nonbeing
- verbal expressions of loneliness:
- "No one really cares."
- "I don't feel like talking."
- "I want to die."
- "Who am I?"

Interventions

- Logo therapy—search for spiritual meaning to illness, life, relationships
- facilitate reflective dialogue on relationships, past and present
- spiritual dialogue on relationships with God, church, world
- offer present of self
- explore relationship with significant others/hospice care staff
- allow opportunity to express feelings of anger, resentment, suicide, and being nobodies in nonjudgmental way
- affirm a transcendent presence that fulfills inner void and gives new meaning to life and relationships

Goals

- feeling of self-acceptance and spiritual solidarity with the divine

Spiritual Sickness: Doubt/Despair

Dying patients may have serious doubts about their supreme being, themselves, and others. This kind of doubt sickens the soul and manifests a crushed faith perspective. Patients with a crushed faith have lost faith and trust in mostly everyone and everything. They have become cynical, negative, and pessimistic.

Need

Dying patients need to express their feelings of doubt and distrust. They must learn to develop a consolidated faith that embraces their suffering and doubts and discovers meaning in it

Symptoms

The dying patient may exhibit the following feelings and behaviors:

- expressing doubt and lack of faith in a supreme being
- feelings of bitterness and resentment
- distrust of some authority figures (i.e. doctor, nurse, clergy, health aides)
- rejection of religious beliefs, institutions, and clergy
- unexplained anger and hostility
- complete withdrawal and rejection of others
- sense of sadness, despair, and dejection

Interventions

The pastor, caregiver, hospice clinician will listen to patient's cynical feelings and story and learn the source of his or her doubts. The will reveal love and heal their brokenness. Finally, they will use Logo therapy to help the patient develop a consolidated faith perspective.

- Listen non judgmentally to all the patient's feelings and doubts.
- Learn from the patient telling his or her story about the source of his or her doubts.
- Love the patient by being trustworthy, consistent, and caring to his or her needs.
- Logo therapy is needed to develop a new meaning in life.

Goal

The pastor, caregiver, hospice clinician's goal is to help the patient work through his or her doubts and develop a sense of inner peace and trust in others and in a supreme being.

Spiritual Sickness: Guilt

Guilt is a feeling arising from a commission or omission of an action thought to be wrong or immoral. Guilt can be real or imagined, rational or irrational.

Need

*   facilitate inner healing, peace of mind, self-forgiveness

Symptoms

*   verbal admission of guilt with identified needs to make amends
*   statements indicating patient/caregiver believes he or she somehow deserve this illness or brought it upon him or herself
*   expression of anger toward the patient's God can sometimes indicate guilt (in transference of feelings)
*   fear of death can reflect a fear of judgment
*   belief that the patient does not deserve the care he or she is receiving
*   bringing up past events, such as divorce or events that may have had a negative influence on the patient's children
*   using words such as excommunication, alienation, rejection, and shunning in relation to the patient's church.

Interventions

- assist patient/caregiver to identify source of guilt and encourage the patient to verbalize (reflective dialogue, which helps patients identify their rational or irrational guilt)
- when patient/caregiver identifies need for amends, assist in identifying ways they may approach this (i.e., face to face, letter writing, prayer/reconciliation)
- when guilt shows itself as a feeling that "I am not good enough" or "I deserve this illness," listen to the patient/caregiver in a nonjudgmental manner, help to identify the source of the feeling, and allow verbalization; facilitate self-acceptance

Goals

- assist in reconciliation through positive affirmation, appropriate spiritual readings
- initiate a dialogue clarifying the patient/caregiver's understanding of guilt and through their faith tradition, diminish irrational guilt

Spiritual Sickness: Alzheimer's/Dementia

Alzheimer's is a progressive mental deterioration that can occur in middle or old age, due generalized degenerate of the brain. Dementia is a brain disease marked by memory disorders, personality changes, and impaired reasoning.

Need

- Affirm feelings, spirit, value, life story and relationships that will give spiritual meaning

Symptoms

- Short-term memory -struggle to remember where they put things and what they are doing
- Boundary effect- forget why they came into a room
- Finding the right words- struggle to speak coherently
- Mood swings- irritability, bouts of depression, anger, and frustration
- Slow movement- slow in speech, thought, moment
- Lethargy- extreme tiredness, disinterest in activities
- Difficult with forward planning- difficulty following a plot to a movie
- Getting lost- go for walks or shopping and get lost
- Struggle to complete ordinary tasks- poor hygiene
- Problems with writing- lose train of thought
- Being repetitive- keep repeating things
- Change in Behavior- acts completely different
- Sundowning syndrome- restlessness, aggression, panic during the early evening, talking loud to themselves, pacing the floor

Interventions

- Ministry of presence- live in the moment, offer yourself, sitting in silence
- Allow opportunity to express feelings of anger, confusion, anxiety, irritability and not be judgmental
- Be willing to assist them in doing simple tasks: feeding, walking, hygiene care, etc.
- Advocate for their rights and needs
- Raise awareness of the Alzheimer's/Dementia symptoms to family, friends, caregivers
- Encourage them to tell their life story
- Use pictures, music, cultural icons and old movies, shows to trigger pleasant memories

- Share familiar biblical stories, hymns, prayers to foster religious memories
- Encourage them to participate in social and religious activities.
- Pray with them or for them

Goal

- Feeling of self-acceptance and appreciation of one's life
- Sense of spiritual solidarity with God and others
- Feeling of contentment and inner peace

CHAPTER

3

SPIRITUAL CARE

Spiritual care addresses the emotional, material, relational, and existential needs and concerns of the patient and his or her family. The essence of spiritual care is not religious but the ability to recognize and respond to the internal exigencies of the dying. Spiritual care is entering the world of the terminally ill and nurturing their souls. It is taking the journey of life alongside the dying person and their family; the journey is not necessarily religious. Not everyone is religious, but everyone is spiritual. Everyone has values, passions, desires, faults, focuses, feelings, family, and faith in something or someone. Soren Kierkegaard is right: "We are not human beings having a spiritual experience. We are spiritual beings having a human experience." We are more than our gender, race, physical attributes, socioeconomic background, religion, family roles, and worldly identities. The essence of who we are is spiritual. We are first and foremost spiritual beings, and the needs of the soul should be our primary concern.

Spirituality versus Religiosity

There is a fundamental difference between religiosity and spirituality. Religion focuses on external dimensions, and spirituality focuses on internal dimensions. Religion is all about rituals, and spirituality is about relationships. Religion is based on an institution, and spirituality is grounded in intuition. Religion is about piety, and spirituality is about passion. Religion emphasizes doctrine, and spirituality emphasizes the divine. Religion is about going to church, and spirituality is discovering the church within.

It is important to make the distinction between religion and spirituality. There are many people who are not religious, but they still have spiritual needs. As a hospice chaplain, I met a man dying of cancer and who said he was an atheist. Moreover, he told me he did not believe in God, church, or life after death. He told the social worker that he did not think that seeing a hospice chaplain would be helpful.

When I went to visit him, I never discussed religion or my own personal faith. What I did do was ask him what he enjoyed doing. He showed me a book of poetry he had been writing. I spent hours reading and reflecting on his poetry, which spoke to his spirituality. Toward the end of his life, he was open to discussing his belief in God.

The key to spiritual care is discovering what is important to the dying and exploring or validating their spirituality with them. The goal of spiritual care is peace or what the Hebrews called *shalom*. Shalom is not just the presence of peace; it is the pursuit of that which is good. It is the integration and harmony of all things. Therefore, those who are rendering spiritual care to the dying are helping them to pursue peace. They are assisting the terminally ill to seek peace within themselves, with God, others, and with death. Often, those struggling with the end of their lives are not at peace and manifest a variety of feelings, beliefs, and behaviors. Their souls reveal their pain in some of the following ways.

- **Anger**- Anger maybe displaced directed toward people, God, and/or circumstances

- **Fear:** What will happen when I die? We are fearful of the dying process and what death means.
- **Hopelessness:** We expressed a crushed faith that manifest itself in doubt and emptiness.
- **Loneliness:** We feel we are all alone in our pain and suffering. We think no one cares or can help us.
- **Guilt:** Sometimes we feel as if we are being punished for our sins, or we feel guilty for the things we completed.
- **Sadness:** We feel sad because of death. We may cry and grieve over impending death.
- **Meaninglessness:** We feel that life has no meaning or purpose. We question the meaning of our suffering and our fundamental beliefs. We are filled with doubt and loss of control.

These are just some of the spiritual pains people will experience during the death and dying process. Elizabeth Keebler-Ross has presented the framework of five stages experienced by the dying person. She states they are denial, anger, bargaining, depression, and acceptance. We may experience some or a combination of these feelings.

How to Give Spiritual Care

The terminally ill require spiritual care that will address the manifold needs of the soul. To give good spiritual care, one does not have to be a hospice chaplain or a clergy person or have special training or achieve a degree. Spiritual care requires one to be motivated by love and reveal a compassionate spiritual commitment to the dying. Spiritual care is not religious care, it deals with the heart, mind, and soul of an individual. It is an inward focus on feelings, values, relationships, and beliefs. Contrary, wise religious care deals with the outward manifestations of one's beliefs, doctrines, and principles. Remember, everyone is not religious, but everyone is spiritual, therefore, spiritual care is not just for pastors, hospice chaplains, and clergy, but grief counselors, social workers, or other professionals too because everyone can love, listen, do a life review, engage in logo therapy and learn or teach others. Everyone has the capacity to render spiritual care to the dying and bring healing to their souls. We might not have the same religion or beliefs, but we can use the same spiritual interventions.

Spiritual Interventions

Listening

The most valuable thing you can do for someone who is dying is to listen. We must be willing to listen to their life stories, hear their complaints, bitterness, sadness, worries, doubts, fears, guilt, and despair. We need to listen to them even when they offend us or say something we radically disagree with. We cannot judge or criticize them with our words, eyes, or demeanor. Listening means having a nonjudgmental, non-critical approach to those who are whispering, speaking, babbling, or even shouting at you. Listening does not mean we accept or affirm everything that is said to us. It does mean that we respect the person's right to express his or her feelings and opinions in their own way. Listening means entering the world of the dying person and nurturing them.

As a hospice chaplain, I had to learn the art of listening. I visited a nursing home where an elderly African American woman was dying and had dementia. I saw her walking down the hallway headed for the front door. She wore a big, wide church hat and a thick wool coat. She was carrying a bag as she waddled down the hallway.

I asked her, "Where are you going?"

She said, "I'm going home, and this is not my home. Now please get out of my way. I got to catch the bus."

So, I moved aside, but I admit I was concerned. I was afraid she would walk outside of the nursing home and get lost somewhere. I walked with her, trying to convince her to turn around and go back to her room. She got to the reception desk and asked the receptionist, "Did the bus get here yet?"

The receptionist smiled and said, "Oh no, you just missed it, but if you want to you can sit down and come back tomorrow."

I asked the receptionist what it was all about. She told me that this precious old woman came to her desk every day and asked if the bus arrived to take her to Atlanta, Georgia. She said she pretended right along with her and acted as if she were at a bus depot. She said she never questioned her or criticized her. She entered her world and supported her. The nursing home receptionist reminded me of what it is to really listen. Listening means entering that person's world and nurturing him or her.

Life Review

A Life Review is when the pastor, hospice clinician, clergy or caregiver encourages the dying person to tell their life story. One can learn a lot of wisdom and truth from by conducting a life review with a dying person. Some of the greatest teachers do not teach at Ivy League schools, colleges, or universities. The most profound teachers are those lying in their beds of afflictions. I have learned more wisdom and truth from dying patients than from any of my Harvard Divinity School teachers. Ralph Waldo Emerson is right: "Every man is my superior in that I may learn from them." If we keep an open mind, we can learn so much from the terminally ill. Life review will not only give wisdom to the hospice clinician it will also give spiritual insight to the dying. The dying will be able to see themselves from a different perspective and rediscover who they were and who they are becoming. Life review enables the dying to come to grips with their strengths and weaknesses. They can learn from their mistakes and take pride in their accomplishments. Reviewing their life will ultimately validate their feelings, thoughts, and beliefs. It will help them to discover what their purpose is in life. Life review will get the dying in touch with what was and what is important to them. They have a story to tell, and we all need to hear it. Many dying people have a strong compulsion to tell their story. They want to tell you about all of their struggles and what they had to do to overcome them. They want to witness to you about what the Lord has done. They want to share what they have been able to accomplish and brag about their achievements. Everyone has a story to tell and a legacy to leave. Many of the dying love to tell their story and have something to teach us. If you are willing to listen, you will not only validate them but will learn in the process.

As a hospice chaplain I had the privilege to hear the life stories of many patients. I will never forget this World War II veteran who was paralyzed from the neck down. He could not move his limbs or his neck. He was a prisoner of his own body. But his spirit soared like a free bird when he began to talk about his life. He asked me to place his pictures on his wall so that he could see them. After I put them on the wall, we spent hours talking about them. He enjoyed talking about his military service. His eyes lit up when reminisced about his deceased wife. He laughed out loud when he remembered some of his blunders. His whole demeanor changed when he reflected on his life. Life review was like medicine to his soul.

Loving

The most spiritual thing that you could do for someone who is dying is love them. The Greek philosophers defined love in three ways.

There is *philia,* which means friendship. In this kind of love, you love those who love you. You help those who help you. Then there is *Eros* love. This is the kind of romantic love between a man and a woman. This is passionate feeling for the beloved. Finally, there is *agape* love. This is the love of God that works in the human heart. This love is not limited only to friends, family, and lovers but is extended to every human being.

Agape love is given to others because God loves them. Agape love is what Paul the apostle wrote about in 1 Corinthians 13. He wrote, "Love suffers long and is kind. Love envies not. Love vaunts not itself and is not puffed up. It doesn't behave itself unseemly, seeks not his own. Love bears all things believes all things, hopes all things, and endures all things. Love never fails" (1 Cor. 13:4–8). Agape love is what is needed by the terminally ill. Many of them feel unloved, unappreciated, and uncared for. Loving people when they are dying may manifest itself in many ways. It may mean holding their hands, feeding them, cleaning them, dressing them, sitting in silence with them, allowing them to vent, reading to them, watching television, listening to music with them, praying with them, swabbing their mouth, combing their hair, playing bingo, attending therapy, laughing, crying, praying for them, and many other things. Loving a person who is dying means to do whatever he or she needs at any given moment.

One of the most loving things one could do for a person who is dying is to provide music therapy. Music therapy is a spiritual intervention that can bring healing to the soul. There is a spirituality in all music that can soothe the heart and mind. Music can reach people in ways that mere words cannot. It can lift the heart and bring back pleasant memories. It can put a smile on your face and tears of joy in your eyes. Music can inspire the physically challenged to do the impossible. It can inspire a sinner to become a saint or motivate the weak to become strong. Music can inspire the terminally ill to face death with grace and courage. It is up to clergy, caregiver or hospice clinician to discover what kind of music the dying person enjoys and provide it for them.

As a hospice chaplain, I have seen dying patients be inspired by music. Some have been inspired by Gospels and Spirituals. Some have found great joy in listening to Classical music. Others have been moved by R&B and even Rap music. One woman I served loved listening to Johnny Cash. She did not want to talk about God, family, faith or anything to do with religion. All she wanted to do was listen to her CD set of Johnny Cash. What was so interesting was how her mood changed when she listened. Most of the time she was tense, sad and withdrawn, but after hearing that distinctive bass baritone voice in the "Ring of Fire" and "I Walk the Line" she was happy, relaxed and sociable. For this woman listening to Johnny Cash was therapeutic experience. If you want to show love let them listen to their music.

Love is such a powerful healing force. Once a person realizes that they are being loved it can transform them. I once knew a woman who felt unloved and unappreciated because none of her three adult children came to visit her, moreover, she had serious doubts about the love of God. One day when I was visiting her she began to complain about being unloved. She said, "Nobody cares for me." Ironically, as she was saying this an aide was tenderly brushing her hair. I said to her, "Isn't it possible that this aide caring for you is a manifestation of Gods' love?" I reminded her that the love of God comes in many ways and through many different people. The patient eyes were open, and she began to see and appreciate Gods love. She no longer complained about her adult children not visiting her. She saw and experienced Gods love every time someone fed her, clothed her, polished her nails and gave her medication, placed her in bed and put her in the wheelchair. She stopped taking the nursing home aides services for granted. She expressed her appreciation to them and to God. This hospice patient had changed her spiritual perspective and felt loved. The fact that she felt loved is what enabled her to cope with her terminality.

Logo therapy

People on their deathbeds often struggle with life's meaning and purpose. At one time in their lives, they may have lived fully with families, careers, and other fulfilling activities, but when the dying are unable to do the things they used to do, they wrestle with their purpose in life. If they are conscious and alert, the pastor, hospice chaplain, clergy, or caregiver may use Logo therapy. Logo therapy was developed by neurologist and psychiatrist Viktor Frankel. Logo therapy is based on existential analysis of focusing on the will to meaning. It is focused on the belief that it is the striving to find meaning in life that is the primary, powerful motivating and driving force in humans. Victor Frankel's book "Will to Meaning" shares these basic tenets:

- Life has meaning even in painful, difficult circumstances.
- Our primary purpose for living is our will to find meaning in life.
- We have freedom to find meaning in what we do and what we experience or at least in the stand we take when faced with a situation of unchangeable suffering.

Logo therapy is especially needed when people are struggling to find meaning in their suffering and terminal illness. Helping people to reflect on making life meaningful in spite of their sickness is critical to their souls' wellbeing. Logo therapy or a reflective conversation can ultimately bring about a sense of acceptance and inner tranquility. It can even mean a fuller life, with purpose and joy.

I will never forget the time I had the opportunity to visit a sixty-five-year-old terminally ill woman at her home. She had just discovered she was going to die and was extremely depressed. She was so full of despair that she shunned all visitors, stayed locked up in her bedroom, and kept all lights off and blinds closed. Her room was dark and dreary. It seemed like a dungeon. There was an atmosphere of hopelessness and emptiness. Her family insisted that I, her pastor, visit her. When I visited her, she barely spoke a word. We sat in silence for a long time.

She broke the silence and said with anger, "It's not fair. It's not fair. I am a Christian. I pray and what good is it? Why am I dying? Why am I suffering? Why am I dying so young in life?"

I shared with her that I didn't have any good answers to her question, however, I did make this statement: "None of us know how long we will live. Any of us could die at any time. So, the question isn't when we are going to die. The question is, what will we do in the meantime? We cannot add more days to our lives, but we can add more life to our days."

We began to reflect on the things she could still do. When I returned to see her, a major transformation had taken place. The lights were not only on in her room, but they were on in her life. She was hopeful and joyful and had a new meaning in life. The dreary, dark room I had once entered, had been transformed into a sanctuary of praise and hope. She had gospel music playing on the radio, the blinds were open, she had a Bible on her bed, and she was singing to the glory of God. I asked her what happened. She said she was reflecting on her life and what she could still do. She exclaimed, "I don't know when I am going to die. But I know that I can still praise and thank God for the life I still have, and I can teach my children and grandchildren how to live and how to die." As a result of our reflective conversation, this woman was able to find new meaning in her life.

Some dying people can discover a new zeal for life when they have discovered their purpose. There was an eighty-four-year-old woman dying of cancer and had become very depressed. She said she felt she no longer had anything to live for. She was ready to die. As I reviewed her life with her she admitted that she had one regret and that was she never owned a home. She had always lived in apartments or with others, and this made her feel like a failure. The more we discussed this the more she wanted to pursue home ownership. She got her family members to take her to look for a home. They did not agree with her search but that did not stop her. Eventually she purchased a home. Interestingly she was no longer depressed and lethargic. The dream of homeownership energized her and made life worth living. She found a reason to live. She spent every waking hour getting her new home repaired. She said, "I might not live a long life in that house, but I will live there." It is an amazing what people will endure when they have a reason to live.

One dying hospice patient said she wanted to stay alive until her grandchild was born. She refused pain medication because she wanted to be alert when her grandchild was born. She endured so much pain and suffering awaiting her grandchild. When her grandchild was born the family brought her to her dying grandmother. The minute they laid the baby on the dying grandmother's shoulder she died. She stayed alive long enough to see her grand baby.

Logo therapy can assist the dying in discovering a reason to die. There was a dying widow who felt hopeless and sad. In our reflective conversation she revealed a crushed faith perspective and had lost faith in religion, church and even God. The death of her husband made her lose faith in everyone and everything. She did not look forward to death because death meant nonbeing and nothingness. As we engaged in reflective conversation, she shared that the only thing that gave her joy was her deceased husband. She loved her husband and desperately missed him. Every day she thought and talked about him. Unfortunately, the more she talked about him the more miserable she felt. What turned her life around was when she found a reason to die. She began to visualize meeting her husband in the afterlife. She thought about the conversation she would have with him. She looked forward to seeing him again. She dreamed of holding her husband's hand as they walked through paradise. She no longer talked about her husband in the past tense. She talked about being with him in the future. For her death was no longer the end of life it was a new beginning. She could not wait to die to be reunited with her husband. When I would visit her, she would smile and say, "I am going to be with him soon. Every day I get closer and closer." This dying widow had found a reason to die and was glad about it.

Some reflective question you might want to ask someone who is dying are:

- What can you do to make your life meaningful?
- How can you still enjoy your life?
- What are some of the things you still can do?
- What kind of attitude do you need to cope with your situation?
- What messages do you want to give your loved ones?
- How can your sickness strengthen or develop your character or faith?

Logo therapy is an excellent spiritual intervention or tool to assist the dying to find meaning and purpose in life. Asking the right questions can unlock the doors of spiritual insight and understanding. It can raise the conscious level of the dying and help them learn more about themselves and God. They will learn what is important and how to still have a meaningful life. The dying can discover inner peace in pursuing their passion. Logo therapy can enable them to understand the redemptive purpose to their pain and suffering. They can realize that their suffering is not in vain and they can transcend it. Logo therapy enlightens the dying to realize that they can choose their own attitude, positively as opposed to a negative one. The dying can choose to thank God for what they have instead of complaining about what they do not have. Logo therapy will assist in developing spiritual practices that will enhance their soul. They will learn what things can be done to build character and prepare them for death.

Learning

The learning or instruction given to the terminally ill is a very important spiritual intervention. There may be some very critical information and insight that the dying may need to hear, read, reflect, learn or meditate on before they die. One word of wisdom may mean the difference between dying with a restless spirit and dying in peace. The right spiritual insight and information can mend a broken heart, heal a wounded spirit, open a closed mind and set free an enslaved soul. Never underestimate the power of the spoken word, it can literally bring life to those who are dying.

The chaplain, clergy, hospice clinician, social worker, bereavement counselor or caregiver may have to provide new learning for the dying and this may come in the form of poetry, religious literature, grief information, meditations, daily devotionals, self-help information, bible reading, inspirational CD's or DVD's, television, movies, literature on a patient's hobbies, music or their own words of wisdom.

As a hospice chaplain, I am always listening to what a patient may want to hear or what their passion is. One patient I served had a passion for antique cars. When he was healthy, he would spend his free time restoring his 1955 XK 140 JAGUAR. He had pictures of his car on his bed stand. Whenever I visited him, he would talk about his jaguar. So, I brought to him a book about restoring jaguar cars. This car book brought a smile to his face. He loved reading it and looking at the pictures. As a result of reconnecting this patient with his passion it enhanced our professional relationship. Consequently, we not only talked about restoring antique cars but restoring his soul. He learned about who he was in relation to God. Learning a hospice patient's hobby and then giving them more information on it can be a source of joy for the patient.

There have been many dying patients who hungered and thirsted for spiritual nourishment. They needed a meditation that would lift their spirits. I have had the opportunity and privilege to read a meditation or a scripture from the bible to the terminally ill. Many of the meditations that I have read to hospice patients are in this book. Their responses have always been positive. One woman on hospice shed tears of joy when I read her several meditations. She said, "I am so thankful to hear that God knows me and God cares." Also reading poetry or the bible can bring a lot of comfort to the dying.

There are times when the spiritual care provider will have to educate the terminally ill and their family in the bereavement process. They need to understand the various feelings, thoughts and behavior they may go through. The spiritual care provider can educate the caregiver on anticipatory grief issues. They can inform them on ways in which they can cope with their dying loved ones. Educating the bereaved is an important service.

There may be dying people who are ignorant about their religious beliefs and doctrines. They may have been raised in a religious tradition but that does not mean they are informed about it. Their lack of religious knowledge may cause some spiritual distress. It is the spiritual care provider's responsibility to educate the patient on their religion and theology. Some terminally ill people may need to be reeducated about their faith so that they can cope with the dying process. Teaching about God, religion, faith development, spiritual practices, theodicy, grace, grief, salvation, spirituality, inner peace, morals and love are just a few of the subjects that the spiritual care counselors may instruct those facing their demise.

CHAPTER

4

SPIRITUAL MEDITATIONS

What do you say to someone who is dying? What words could you say that would mend their broken heart, heal their wounded spirit and give peace to their troubled soul? Is there a word of hope and encouragement for those who are confronted with the end of their life? Is there something that can be said to someone who is afraid to die? What do you say to those who have become bitter and angry with the prospect of dying? Is there a message for the dying person who has lost their faith in God? What do you say to someone who does not believe in God? How does the clergy person comfort the unbeliever? When tears are falling and gloom fills the room, what does the pastor, chaplain, hospice clinician, social worker, nurse or grief counselor, caregiver say to the dying person? How do you fulfill those long, lonely silent hours?

Hopefully, these spiritual meditations will answer these inquiries and be a helpful resource to pastors, nurses, hospice clinicians, social workers, clergy, grief counselor and caregivers. All of those who are caring for the dying will be able to read these meditations and give comfort. Each spiritual meditation is based on a quote, followed by a brief prayer and reflective questions that can stimulate a spiritual dialogue. Both the spiritual care provider and the terminally ill can be inspired by them.

These spiritual meditations address a wide variety of feelings and perspectives. They will validate and comfort those who have feelings of anger, despair, guilt, sadness fear, anxiousness, hopelessness, bitterness, regret, doubt, confusion, loneliness and meaninglessness. Some of the meditations will strengthen those who are weak in the faith and affirm the constant care and compassion of God. Their faith and trust in God will be renewed. There are meditations that will bring a sense of joy and gratitude to the dying. They will become more appreciative for all the blessings of life. There are meditations that will challenge their earthly provincial perspectives, transform and renew their minds for the next life. Lastly, there are meditations that will inspire the dying to live their life to the fullest. They will be encouraged to have a positive attitude and be encouraged to make the most out of their life. All these meditations, prayers and reflective questions will ultimately give the terminally ill a sense of peace. It matters not whether a dying person is alert and able to verbally respond or is nonverbal and non-responsive, these meditations will fulfill the spiritual needs of the soul.

OPEN THE DOOR TO JOY

"They that sow in tears shall reap in joy." (Psalm 126:5)

The other side of sorrow and sadness is joy and gladness. Every tear that you shed is reflective of the enormous happiness that you possess. You cannot have joy without sorrow, they are two sides of the same coin. We need them both to survive the grieving process and to grow in grace.

As we cry, we are releasing our pain and suffering. We must express our hurt if we are to experience joy again. Our grieving becomes a door for joy to enter. If we withhold our tears, we are also preventing this form from happening. Some people think repressing sorrow will lead to peace, on the contrary, withholding tears only increases inner turmoil and despair. The best way to open the door to joy is by grieving. Let your tears flow. Allow yourself the time and space to express yourself. As you grieve, you will discover that your healing process will begin. The wounds that are on your hearts will slowly be healed, you will begin to smile again. The scars that are on your mind will be mended. Those painful memories will no longer overshadow your thinking process. After a while, you will rediscover joy again. An unshakeable joy that no one or nothing can take from you

PRAYER

> O 'Lord my grief and sorrow are too much to bear. My heart breaks and my tears are overflowing. Please heal me of all my sadness. Dry my tears and heal my broken heart that I may experience your joy. Grant me a joy that the world cannot give, and the world cannot take away. Amen

REFLECTIVE QUESTIONS

1. What makes you sad? What gives you joy?
2. How is God healing your broken heart?
3. How can you give comfort to those grieving?
4. Do you give yourself time to grieve?
5. What do you think about people who grieve openly?
6. Can a person be strong and still cry? Why or why not?
7. Healing is a process. Are you at the beginning, middle or the end of the healing process?
8. What thoughts give you peace?

9. What can you do to help yourself grieve?
10. What can you do to give yourself joy?
11. If you cry does that make you feel weak?
12. Are you afraid to let yourself go emotionally? Why?

MORNING JOY

*"Weeping may endure for a night but joy cometh
in the morning." (Psalm 30:5)*

There is a period in our grieving process in which we feel as if we are experiencing what St. John the Cross called, "The Dark Night of our Soul". It is a time of complete despair and desolation. We cannot see any hope for today or tomorrow. It may seem as if there is no reason to live and our sorrow seems endless. It appears as if the hurt will never go away, however, every dark night ultimately gives way to morning. Morning Joy comes when you have endured the long, lonely nights of grief. It comes with the realization that the night is temporary, and it cannot withstand the soul's natural sunrise. Morning Joy comes when we accept our losses and choose to experience joy anyhow. Our nights are as long as we want them to be. There is a sunrise in your soul. You can choose to see it if you want to. You can choose to be happy despite death and dying. Morning will come when you choose to see life's positives instead of negatives. It comes when you begin to count your blessings. The more thankful you are the more the darkness gives way to the light. So, let the light shine that you may experience Morning Joy.

REFLECTIVE QUESTIONS

1. What are some things you can be thankful for?
2. How is God blessing you right now?
3. How is it midnight in your life?
4. What are some of the positive things in your life?
5. How is it morning in your life?

PRAYER

*Almighty God, I thank you for preserving me through the night.
Amen*

JOURNEY TO JOY

"Therefore, the redeemed of the Lord shall return, and come to with singing unto Zion, and everlasting joy shall be upon their heads; they shall obtain gladness and joy; and sorrow and mourning shall flee away." (Isaiah 51:11)

The journey from the land of lamentation to the habitat of happiness is one we can take if we choose to. It is an inner journey filled with valleys of despair, and mountains of misery. Your valleys may be deep and filled with despair, but you can climb out of them. Your mountains may be high, but you can either climb them or tunnel through them. Each part of the journey that you overcome, grants you a sense of accomplishment and joy. It will not be easy, but it can be done, and the spiritual reward is a celebration of life. So, keep on walking with God and know that He is with you in every step of the journey. He is with you in the valley and will heal your broken heart. God is with you when you climb life's mountains and will keep your feet from falling. No matter where you are on this journey you can be comforted by the fact that God is with you. His presence alone gives you peace and joy.

REFLECTIVE QUESTIONS

1. Do you feel as if you are in a valley of despair or confronting a mountain of misery? Why?
2. Do you experience the presence of God? Why or why not?

PRAYER

Almighty God I praise you for leading me through this journey. I thank you for granting me the strength and the grace to get through this journey and giving me joy. I know that you are with me in every step of the journey. As long as you walk with me I will know your joy.

YOU HAVE THE VICTORY

"Where, O death, is thy sting? O grave, where is thy victory?" (I. Corinthians 15:55)

It appears as if death will have the victory. There is sadness and despair. Friends and family try to hold back the tears. Everyone seems depressed and hopeless. No one speaks of dying. Everyone is afraid to admit that death is imminent and will overwhelm them. Death has a way of wiping the smile from our faces and stealing our joy. Death has a way of making you feel defeated, worthless and helpless.

Death does not have to have the final say over your life, God does. Contrary to conventional thinking, death is not the end of life, it is the beginning of eternal life, it is a door that leads into a whole new existence full of love, peace and joy. Death is a powerless enemy that is no match for our mighty God. If death was a wrestler, God has pinned him to the mat of life. If death was a runner, then God has out run him to the finish line. If death was a football defensive man, then God broke his tackle and scored a touchdown. If death was a baseball pitcher, then God hit a grand slam and won the game. If death was a hockey player than God scored a hat trick in the third quarter. If death was a basketball player than God did a slam dunk and won, the game. No matter how you look at death it does not have the victory, it is doomed for defeat. We are on the right team and serve the right God. God has given us the victory through His son Jesus Christ. It is through Him and with Him that we have victory over sickness, sorrow, sin and death. We need not despair. The victory is ours. All we need to do is let death take its course and usher us into victory.

PRAYER

O' God I feel defeated, demoralized and depressed. It seems as if life is slowly slipping away from me. I feel as if I have nothing to look forward to. Please give me faith to claim victory during defeat and life during death. Grant me the grace to realize that I already have the victory through our Lord and Savior Jesus Christ. Amen

REFLECTIVE QUESTIONS

1. Do you feel victorious or defeated? Why do you feel this way?
2. How does God give you the victory?
3. What is a victorious attitude?
4. How does physical death mean spiritual victory?
5. What is a defeatist attitude?
6. How does a dying savior on the cross symbolize victory?
7. How does the resurrection of Jesus Christ give you the victory?

DON'T LOSE HEART

"I had fainted, unless I had believed to see the goodness of the Lord in the land of the living. Wait on the Lord; be of good courage, and He shall strengthen thine heart; wait, I say, on the Lord!" (Psalm 27:13-14)

It is so easy to lose heart when death is imminent. Seeing a loved one dying before your very eyes is a hard thing to accept. Their physical deterioration and mental debilitation can be a very sad, depressing sight. The remembrance of their former strength seems to accentuate the enormity of the loss. There is nothing worse than seeing yourself die. It is depressing.

However, we need not lose heart, during all the pain and suffering is a blessing. Despite the enormous losses, there are gains to be experienced, do not lose heart. God is present in every difficult circumstance. He promises never to leave or forsake us. If you look with eyes of faith, you can see his goodness and mercy. You can find meaning in the dying process. You can see God at work in your life and in the life of others. He is there giving you the strength to grieve and wiping the tears from your eyes. You can see His goodness all around you. It is in the caring concerned look on the faces of family and caregivers. It is in the medical treatment provided. It is in the dawning of a new day and the setting of the sun. Do not lose heart God is right there.

<u>REFLECTIVE QUESTIONS</u>

1. Describe some of the ways in which you see God at work in your life?
2. How do you feel when you realize God's presence?
3. Count your blessings. What are you thankful for?

PRAYER

Thank you, God, for your presence, for your power and for your love. AMEN

TESTED BY FIRE

"That the trial of your faith, being much more precious than gold that perisheth, though it be tried with fire, might be found unto praise and honor, and glory at the appearing of Jesus Christ" (I. Peter 1:7)

Sickness, suffering, loneliness and the dying process can be considered a spiritual test that develops our souls and prepares them for glory. It is not the kind of test that we could either pass or fail. God has not created us and allow us to suffer so that we can feel miserable and loose our salvation. It is an examination, a test, a refining process to purify our souls and make them become more and more like God. Trials and tribulations are the fiery crucible that God uses to strengthen our faith, bolster our hope and enliven our love. At the end of this divine process, we shall give God the praise, honor and glory for his mercy and goodness. You are tested by the fire but you shall come forth as pure gold.

Your soul is more precious, more valuable than gold. Every ache and pain, every draining therapy session, every tearful and anguish cry is a fire that purifies the gold of your soul. You can rejoice and be thankful that everyday your soul gets better and better.

REFLECTIVE QUESTIONS

1. How do you feel about being tested and why?
2. What are the ways that you are developing, growing by this test?

PRAYER

God, I am being tested, examined, and challenged by this experience. Please give me the faith, patience and grace to get through this testing period and grow by it. Help me to understand and accept that this painful experience is being used to purify my soul that I may come forth as pure gold. Amen

GOOD BEDSIDE MANNER

"The Lord will strengthen him on his bed of languishing; thou wilt will make all his bed in his sickness." (Psalm 41:3)

Good bedside manner is a rarity nowadays. They are very few people who can tend to all the needs of the dying with sensitivity and compassion. Often healthcare workers are so overworked that they do not have the time or the patience to adequately respond to all your concerns. Even the best physicians, nurses, home health aides, social workers, chaplains and family members are unable to fulfill the exigencies of the soul.

It is good news to know that the Lord has good bedside manner. He is sympathetic, sensitive, caring and compassionate. The Lord understands what you are going through because He went through it Himself. Jesus knows what it is to suffer and to slowly die. He knows what it feels like to be rejected, insulted and ignored while dying. He has had cruel and uncaring people watch him die. Whatever you are going through He has already gone through it.

Therefore, when you cry out to Him know that He hears you and will respond. He is always there to hear your prayers. If He does not alleviate your suffering right away, He will give you the grace to bear it. Like Paul the apostle you will be able to say, "His grace is sufficient." The Lord promises to sustain and strengthen you on your bed of illness. Your body may remain weak, but your soul will be strong. Your flesh may fail you, but your faith will still give you the victory. So, take courage and seek the Lord. He has good bedside manner.

PRAYER

Lord, my God, my Holy physician, please visit me on my bed of affliction and strengthen my soul. Grant me the grace and the faith to experience your presence and power. Amen

REFLECTIVE QUESTIONS

1. What does good bedside manner mean to you and have you received it?
2. How has the Lord given you good bedside manner?
3. How can you give good bedside manner to someone?

WHAT HAS HE DONE?

"Who forgives all thine iniquities, who healeth all thy diseases, who redeemeth thy life from destruction, who crowneth thee with loving-kindness and tender mercies, who satisfieth thy mouth with good things, so that thy youth is renewed like the eagles?" (Psalm 103:3-5)

What has he done for me, said the angry elderly woman dying of a terminal illness? She was thin and frail but managed to sit up and express her anger. She glared at me with her blue eyes and frowned at me and said, "I used to pray to Him, I used to faithfully go and work in the church and for what?! Look at me! I can't walk. I can't do the things that I used to do and I am a prisoner in this damn nursing home!" I let the woman continue to rant and rave. She was very angry, and she had the right to express her anger.

After she vented her anger, I read Psalm 103:3-5. I reminded the woman that God sacrificed His son Jesus Christ to suffer die on the cross for our redemption. It was through His martyrdom that all our sins are forgiven, we are saved from eternal damnation and we receive everlasting life. So, the question is not what has God done? The question is what has God not done? God has done so much for us. We must never forget that he has forgiven us of all our sins and shortcomings. He has rescued us from the fiery flames of hell. He has satisfied our hungry souls with His Holy Spirit. He has promised us eternal life, a robe of righteousness, a crown of life and a mansion in glory. The threat of death cannot diminish or destroy all the many blessings that we have.

There was a look of serenity and calm on the woman's face. She was no longer angry or bitter with God. In fact, she smiled and said, "I never thought about it like that. You're right God has done a lot for me. I guess I need to count my blessings." We prayed together thanking God for all of his blessings.

PRAYER

God you have been good to me. Help me to be more appreciative of all the things that you have done for me. Grant me a grateful spirit that I may give you praise and glory Amen

REFLECTIVE QUESTIONS

1. What has God done for you?
2. Is there anything that you are angry, disappointed or frustrated about?
3. What are some of the things that you are thankful for?
4. How can you have a more positive attitude?

YOU NEED HELP

"Is any sick among you? Let him call for the elders of the church and let them pray over him anointing him with oil in the name of the Lord. And the prayer of faith shall save the sick, and the Lord will raise him up. And if he has committed sins, he will be forgiven." (James 5:14-15)

I stood knocking at his door waiting to be invited in his room. He was a fifty-five-year-old heavy set African American male who had just been diagnosed with an incurable disease. His wife was a member of my church and asked if I would go and visit him. He never attended any church and I was told that he did not believe in God. My knocking on his door seemed to disturb him. He laid in the bed and looked at me with complete disdain on his face. His male friends were standing around his bed and glaring at me. He finally asked me to come in and inquired," who are you and what do you want? I responded, "I am Rev. White and your wife asked me to pray for you." Suddenly, he and his friends started laughing. "What are you supposed to do heal me? He said with a laugh. His friends chuckled. He looked at me with a smirk on his face and said, "Ok go ahead and pray." I knelt beside his bed and petition God to heal him. After I finished praying, I got up and saw that this big, tough man was crying like a baby. Somehow, someway God had penetrated this proud, hard hearted atheist and humbled his soul. All the laughter and false bravado had left the room. All these boisterous macho men became silent in the presence of the Holy Spirit. The only thing that the ill man could say to me is, "Thank you ... I really appreciate your prayer." I told him, "It's alright. I am here for you and God is here for all of us because we all need help." Later, I learned that he was never the same.

We all need help. It does not matter how strong, religious, intelligent, wise or independent you are, you need help. You need to be humble enough to receive assistance from anyone who is willing to give it. The true test of whether someone is strong is whether they realize their own weaknesses. To be strong is to be wise and humble enough to ask for help. So, if you have a need do not sit there in silence. Tell somebody that you need help, and when the help comes be open enough to receive it.

PRAYER

Almighty God, I need your help. I cannot do this alone. Rescue me from my pride and arrogance and heal me in your own way and in your own time. Amen

REFLECTIVE QUESTIONS

1. What do you need help in?
2. What inhibits you from asking for help?
3. How is God helping you?
4. Are you too proud to ask for help?
5. Do you realize that God can work through anybody?
6. What do you need to do to be open to others?
7. Can you see the grace of God in others?
8. Are you open to asking strangers for help? Why or why not?

CHANGE YOUR CLOTHES

"To appoint unto them that mourn in Zion, to give unto them beauty for ashes, the oil of joy for mourning, the garment of praise for the spirit of heaviness; that they may be called trees of righteousness, the planting of the Lord, that He might be glorified." (Isaiah 61:3)

God comforts our afflicted souls by beautifying us with His presence; provides us with joy and strength with His power. God can transform your depressed, distraught demeanor into a countenance of gladness and praise.

To allow God's presence and power to permeate your being is like taking off all tattered clothing and putting on brand new clothes. New clothes can make you look good and you feel good. It is the same for spiritual clothes. Changing spiritual clothes means changing your attitude. We have a choice in our grieving process, we can either keep the clothes of despair on or change into God's garments of praise. Despite all that you are going through you can still thank and praise God for this experience. Maybe you have been wearing the clothing of sadness for too long. Maybe you have been feeling too sorry for yourself. Maybe it is time to change your clothes. You can choose to put on the garments of praise and be thankful for who you are and what God has done for you. Whether you realize it or not you wear the robe of righteousness and the crown of life. Beneath your physical appearances you are wearing the clothing of God. So, take off those clothes of complaints and reveal the garments of praise.

REFLECTIVE QUESTIONS

1. What kind of clothes are you wearing now? The garment of praise or clothes of despair.
2. If you wear the garments of praise, what kind of attitude, demeanor, thoughts, perspective

Or lifestyle should you have?

3. How is wearing the clothes of complaints damaging to your soul?

PRAYER

Dear God, help me to change my clothes. I no longer want to wear the clothes of sadness. Help me to take them off and put on the garments of praise. Help me to find joy in spite of my sorrow. Amen.

SECRET PLACE

"He that dwelleth in the secret place of the Most High shall abide under the shadow of the Almighty". (Psalm 91:1)

There is a secret place for you to go to be protected and comforted through the storms of life. It is a place of refreshment and revitalization. It is a place where you can go to gain a new perspective on your situation. This secret place resides within the heart of every believer. No one knows when you are within your secret place. You could be in a crowd or all alone. You could be in the church or on the street. The secret place is where you have hidden all your real feelings and thoughts. No one knows how you really feel but God. Once you commune with God and share with Him your troubles, you have found your secret place. At that time and place, He will grant you peace. In difficult times, you need to go to the secret place. It is the only place that you can go to feel safe and secure. God has a way of making you feel that He is protecting and strengthening you. Nothing and no one can disturb you in the secret **place.** It is a place of impenetrable peace. It is a place of inner tranquility that no one or nothing can disrupt. To go to the secret place, you must take time to pray and talk to God. You will discover that He is waiting in the secret place. God wants you to share all your worries and sorrows. You can trust Him. He will listen to everything you have to say. Go to the secret place and talk to your God. He is waiting for you.

REFLECTIVE QUESTIONS

1. Have you discovered your secret place with God?
2. How often do you pray?
3. Have you told God how you really feel and what you think? Why or why not?
4. Do you have daily devotional lifestyle?
5. Have you taken time to thank and praise God?

6. Have you taken time to confess your sins and shortcomings to him?
7. Have you taken time to have quiet time with God to listen to Him?

PRAYER

Dear God, I want to spend more quality time with you in the Secret Place. I want us to discover your peace, love sense of security and strength. Amen.

SECOND WIND

"He giveth power to the faint, and to them that have no might, he increaseth strength. Even the youths shall faint and be weary, and the young men shall utterly fall. But they that wait upon the Lord, shall renew their strength, they shall mount up with wings like eagles, they shall run and not be weary, they shall walk and not faint." (Isaiah 40:29-31)

The struggle for life and death is liken to a long-distance race. A long-distance race is physically, mentally, and emotionally draining for even the most able runners.

No matter how religious and or spiritual you are, when you are during a life and death struggle, it can take all the strength and vitality from you. Death can sap all your energy. You become so tired and so weak that you do not have the power to do the simplest task. Sometimes it seems as if you cannot go on. You feel like giving up, you feel like quitting.

It is at those times that you must learn to wait on God to get your second wind. You must accept the fact that it is natural for the body to get weak. It is understandable for you to feel like giving up, but, you do not have to give in to your feelings. You can choose to walk by faith and trust that God will give you the inner strength to go on. God will give you second wind. Your second wind comes when you rely more on God than yourself. It comes when you see Him as the source of your peace, joy and hope. Depend on God and get your second wind.

REFLECTIVE QUESTIONS

1. Are you feeling tired and what is draining you?
2. Have you begun to rely more on Gods strength to get your second wind?

PRAYER

Almighty God, please give me a Second Wind. Grant me the strength and the power to run this race. Sometimes I feel like giving up; but Lord You and You alone can give me the grace to run and finish the race. Amen.

JOY IN JESUS

"Beloved, think it not strange concerning the fiery trial which is to try you, as though some strange thing happened unto you; but rejoice inasmuch as ye are partakers of Christ's sufferings, that when His glory shall be revealed, ye may be glad with exceeding joy." (I. Peter 4:12, 13)

Sometimes we assume that our faith in God and exemplary behavior should exempt us from diseases, suffering and unexpected troubles, but, the Gospel of Jesus Christ does not support that religious illusion. On the contrary, the Gospel of Jesus Christ instructs us that suffering, pain, problems, are a way of life. It is in this experience that we can discover the joy of Jesus. It is joy that is found during our cross. We share our cross with our God. When we cry, He cries with us, our sorrows are His sorrows. The joy is not in the cross itself or in the terminal illness. The joy is that we share our cross with our lord. Bearing it can be a source of joy.

It is in our cross that we fully immerse ourselves in God's presence. It is in God's presence that we discover a sense of serenity and indescribable joy.

Moreover, the tears that you shed and the sorrow that you feel is nothing compared to the eternal joy that you will have. God promises you eternal life and in that life, there is not any sickness, sorrow or death. There is nothing but peace, joy, love and righteousness. You may cry today but tomorrow there will be joy. One day you will be living in heaven with all the saints and angels praising our God. You will celebrate and rejoice that your suffering has ended. You will be praising God for delivering your soul. It will be a new beginning with a new life and new wonderful experiences.

REFLECTIVE QUESTIONS

1. How do you feel about what you are going through?
2. Do you believe that God understands and accepts how you feel?
3. What kind of feelings will you have in heaven?
4. How is Jesus giving you joy?

PRAYER

Almighty merciful God, please be merciful to me during my suffering. Grant me the vision to see past this veil of tears and visualize a future of eternal bliss. Help me to find joy in this present moment and in the next life. Amen.

WHO ARE YOU WAITING FOR?

"Wait on the Lord; be of good courage, and He shall strengthened thine heart; wait, I say, on the Lord" (Psalm 27:14)

One of the most debilitating experiences one can encounter is waiting for someone or for something to happen. Waiting can be emotionally draining, psychologically destabilizing, and spiritually eroding. Waiting for the health care clinicians to come and give you care can produce a great deal of anxiety. Busy health care workers rarely come on schedule and when they do, it may seem too brief.

Waiting for loved ones to arrive and give a word of comfort can sometime be a disappointing experience. Sometimes, they arrive late and often they say the wrong thing. Besides, they have a life of their own.

Those who wait on the Lord will discover that God is a doctor who can heal a sin sick soul. Whatever frustrations, fears, sadness or bitterness that plagues the soul can be eradicated by God's presence. When we wait on God, he strengthens our weakened souls. Those who wait on the Lord will discover that "he is a friend that sticketh closer than a brother". Jesus is our family. He will be a parent, a sibling, a friend, a spouse that will never leave you nor forsake you. There is no greater love than the love of God.

The next time that you feel anxious as you wait for someone, remember to wait on the Lord. He is always there, and He is always on time. He will strengthen your heart.

REFLECTIVE QUESTIONS

1. Who or what have you been waiting for?
2. How do you feel when you are waiting?
3. What Could you do while you wait??

4. What does it mean to "wait on the Lord"?
5. What are the benefits to waiting on the Lord?

PRAYER

Almighty, all wise God you are the Alpha and the Omega; the beginning and the end. You have all time in your hands. Help me to be patient and trust you. Grant me the grace and patience to wait on you. Amen

LOOK IN THE MIRROR

"But, let everyone prove his own work, and then shall he have rejoicing in himself alone, and not in another." (Galatians 6:4)

Self-reflection and spiritual introspection are like looking at the mirror of your soul. Experiencing terminal illness can lead you to reflect on your past and present. It is time to look in the mirror and reassess who you were, what you have become and what are your possibilities.

As you reflect on your history you may remember something that you said or did that was shameful... You may have some regrets about your faults and failures. It is time to discover the joy that comes with forgiving yourself and others. God is full of mercy and grace and accepts us as we are. You must do the same and accept yourself.

Furthermore, look in the mirror of your soul and see the presence of God. You are becoming more and more like God's child. Look beyond the worry and anguish on your face and see the grace and the glory of God. God is in you. His powerful presence radiates within your soul. Look in the mirror and you will discover a divine identity that gets more and more beautiful every day. God forgives you of your past and has a glorious future for you. Take a long look into the mirror and you will discover that you are fearfully and wonderfully made. You are a child of God and you look good!

REFLECTIVE QUESTIONS

1. What are some of the things that you have done that you regret?
2. Have you forgiven yourself? Why not?
3. What are some things that others have done to you or not done for you that?

4. Have hurt you in the past?
5. Have you forgiven them? Why?
6. Do you love yourself as God loves you?
7. What are some of the things that you could do or say that shows self-love?
8. What are some of the things that you could do or say to improve yourself?
9. When you look in the mirror, do you see the image of God? Why or why not?

PRAYER

Dear God, I thank you that I am made in your image. I praise you that I am fearfully and wonderfully made. Help me to see past all my faults and failures and see the image of your son etched on my soul. Help me to grow in grace and become more and more like you. Amen

GOD KNOWS

"I will be glad and rejoice in thy mercy, for thou hast considered my trouble. Thou hast known my soul in adversities." (Psalm 31:7)

God knows what you are going through and how difficult it is for you. He understands your pain and inner turmoil. He is aware of your bitter disappointments, broken heart and utter despair. God knows you and God cares.

Let the awareness of God's love and constant care be the source of your joy. You can be happy in the fact that God is merciful and knows how much you can bear.

You may think that your cross is too much, but God knows better. He is being extremely merciful. He knows how much you can bear. He knows how you feel. He has felt your pain and experienced your loss. He knows what it is to feel rejected, isolated and alienated. He knows what it is to be lonely. God knows what it is to have life slowly ebb from your being. He knows what it is like to die a painful death. He has experienced what it is like to die young with dreams unfulfilled. He knows what it is like to watch helplessly as your loved one cry before you. God knows and God cares. It is because God knows that He not only can empathize with you but, He can give you the inner strength that you need. God knows how to heal your wounded spirit and strengthen your weakened soul. You can take courage in the fact that God knows!

REFLECTIVE QUESTIONS

1. Do you feel that you are isolated, desolated and along in your suffering?
2. Do you feel as if nobody cares?
3. How do you feel knowing that God cares?
4. Have you shared how you feel to God?

PRAYER

God of comfort and grace, I thank you for your knowledge of me. I praise you for knowing all my burdens, pains and problems. I glorify you because you are Omniscient, all knowing, all powerful God who cares deeply about me.

WEEP NO MORE

"For the people shall dwell in Zion at Jerusalem; thou shalt weep no more. He will be very gracious unto thee at the voice of thy cry; when He shall hear it, He will answer thee." (Isaiah 30:19)

Tears are a very natural and healthy aspect of human suffering. In fact, the inability to cry may be a sign of emotional illness. Tears have a way of cleansing the soul of its sorrow. So, it is important to cry when we feel like it.

There will also be a time when you will no longer cry. There will be a point in your life when "you shall weep no more". God can dry the tears from your eyes and end your grief. It is not in His will for you to grieve forever. He does not want your life to be one endless tear after another.

Every time you cry out and shed a tear, He hears you. God will answer your prayer. He will fulfill your needs. He will wipe your tears away. He will give you the inner strength to weep no more. It is possible to no longer grieve over the loss or the impending loss of a loved one. God can grant you the grace to grieve and be at ease. He can give you a sense of contentment. Truly, life will not be the same after your loved one dies, and God is able to empower you to go on with your life. God can make your life worth living again. You might not believe it now because you are hurting so much, but, one day you will weep no more.

REFLECTIVE QUESTIONS

1. What are you crying about?
2. Why do you think it is healthy to cry?
3. Do you believe that God can wipe away your tears?
4. How is God answering your prayers today?
5. Have you prayed to God and shared your feelings?

PRAYER

God of Comfort allow me the strength to be weak, the faith to be afraid, the peace to have turmoil. Allow me to see that there is healing as I share my sorrow. Please wipe the tears from my eyes. Amen

I CAN

*"I can do all things through Christ who
strengthens me." (Philippians 4:13)*

I can still experience joy instead of sorrow.

I can still receive and give love.

I can choose a life of faith and courage over fear.

I can choose hope over despair and apathy.

I can still experience the abundance of life despite physical illness,
financial hardships, emotional difficulties or other limitations.

I can believe despite unanswered prayer and deferred dreams.

I can climb any mountain, bear any cross, stand during a storm,
endure any pain, survive any sickness, triumph over any tragedy and
cope with any crises. I can live now and after I die. With Christ I
can do all things!

<u>REFLECTIVE QUESTIONS</u>

1. What do you have doubts about?
2. Why do you have these doubts?
3. Have you asked God to help you with your self-doubts?
4. Are you aware that you have the option to respond positively
   to your situation?
5. What or who do you place your confidence in?

PRAYER

Almighty God forgive me for doubting you and your divine power inside of me. Help me to discover inner strength to conquer my circumstances. Amen

YOU ARE A MASTERPIECE

"Being confident of this very thing, that he which hath God begun a good work in you will perform it until the day of Jesus Christ." (Philippians 1:6)

One day, the great sculptor Michael Angelo was dragging a marble rock through a village and someone asked him, "What are you going to do with that rock"? Michael Angelo fired back, "That's no rock, and it is a masterpiece! In this rock is a masterpiece!"

God looks upon each of us as His masterpiece. To the world we may not look like much, but God sees the greatness in us. You are God's masterpiece.

Sometimes it takes sickness and long suffering to shape the soul into a more perfect image of God. Life's disappointments, diseases, brokenness, and burdens have a way of drawing us closer to the Sculptor of our souls. Consequently, our faith gets shaped, our hearts get more sensitive and our minds become more centered on holy things. You are God's masterpiece. Allow Him to shape you into His image. Let His tender touch chip away the sins from your soul. Let go of any bad attitudes that you have. Yield yourself to this divine process of purification and holiness. It may be painful, but you will be a masterpiece, a handiwork of a Mighty God.

REFLECTIVE QUESTIONS

1. How can you see this experience as a way of making you a better person?
2. What are the ways that God is making you stronger in your faith or larger in love?
3. What is preventing you from yielding yourself to this divine metamorphosis?

PRAYER

Creator God, I pray that you will use this difficult experience to make me a better child of yours. I surrender myself to you because I trust your handiwork. Mold me, make me, and shape me according to your will that I may glorify you. Amen.

THE JOY OF WAITING

"And it will be said in that day, lo this is our God; we have waited for Him and He will save us. This is the Lord; we have waited for Him; we will be glad and rejoice in His salvation" (Isaiah 25:9)

She was a frail, skeletal, 85-year-old woman, slowly deteriorating and dying of cancer. She had a lot of difficulty breathing which made it hard for her to sleep and talk. Yet despite her pain and suffering, was able to praise and thank the Lord. I asked her "what do you do all day?" She said, "I am waiting on the Lord to take me home...I trust God knows the right time and when He comes, I'll be ready." I inquired, "Don't you get tired of waiting?" She uttered, "Oh no, I find joy in just praising and thanking Him for being so good to me. I just reflect on all of His goodness and what He's done for me in the past." This dear elderly woman discovered joy that comes in waiting on the Lord. Her jubilant spirit was like to a little girl waiting for Christmas day. Like a child, she was anxiously anticipating the greatest gift of all time—eternal life in Christ.

REFLECTIVE QUESTIONS

1. Are you tired of waiting?
2. Are there more spiritually productive ways that you could spend your time?
3. What is God doing for you now?
4. Can you thank and praise God while you wait on Him?
5. What does it mean to wait on God?

PRAYER

Lord, I thank and praise you for all that you have done for me. I cannot count all your blessings. They are too numerous for me. As I wait for you, I will praise you. Amen

HE IS IN YOU

"Ye are of God, little children, and have overcome them, because greater is he that is in you than he that is in the world." (I. John 4:4)

Life is full of obstacles, sickness, suffering, financial crises, disappointments, deferred dreams, diseases and terminality. Once we have coped with one obstacle, it seems as if another comes to confront us. In a sense, we are hurdlers who must jump one hurdle after another. The only way we can rise above each obstacle is to remember that we are children of God. As children of God, we have the inherent ability to overcome our obstacles. In each of us is the resurrected Spirit of Christ that cannot be suppressed, downtrodden or hemmed in.

We can rise above it all to the glory of God. Nothing or no one can bring us down. Every obstacle is an opportunity for us to overcome. The one who is in you is greater than anything outside of you. So, keep the faith and know that you can handle anything that comes your way.

REFLECTIVE QUESTIONS

1. What are some of the specific obstacles that you are encountering?
2. How can you effectively cope with your obstacles?
3. How has God helped you to overcome past obstacles?
4. How is God helping you now to overcome your obstacles?

PRAYER

Lord you have overcome sin, suffering, death and the devil. You are the ultimate over comer, victor and triumphant God. I thank you that the same spirit that you had to overcome the world is the same spirit that I have. It is because you have overcome obstacles, I can overcome my obstacles. Thank you, Lord. Amen.

SONG OF JOY

"Let the saints be joyful in glory; let them sing aloud on their beds. Let the high praises of God be in their mouth, and a two-edged sword in their hand." (Psalm 149:6)

She was terminally ill and had suffered from a stroke which made her mouth droop down, yet, she sang from the depths of her heart, "Blessed Assurance, Jesus is mine. Oh, what foretaste of glory divine. Heir of salvation, purchase of God, born of His spirit, washed in His blood. This is my story, this is my song, praising my Savior all day long."

She would not stop singing. She said she used to sing in her church choir, but she was getting ready to sing in God's heavenly choir. She had a song of joy to sing and so do you. If this sick woman could sing so can you. God has given you a song to sing. It may be a song of peace or of joy. It may be a song of victory or of love. Whatever your song is sing it to the glory of God. Sing your song until the day you find yourself in Gods celestial choir. Never forget you do not sing to please others but you sing to please your God.

REFLECTIVE QUESTIONS

1. What is your song and are you singing it? Why or why not?
2. How do you think you would feel if you began singing to God?

PRAYER

Lord, give me a song, a song to praise you. A song to glorify you. A song that tells of your loveliness, of your grace and mercy. Let me sing so that even the angels will stop and listen and praise you. Amen.

WHAT SHALL I RENDER?

"By Him therefore let us offer the sacrifice of praise to God continually, that is, the fruit of our lips, giving thanks to His name." (Hebrew 13:15)

What shall I render to my God? What do you do when you no longer have the physical mobility to go to church and serve Him with your talents, gifts and abilities? What can you give to God when you are dying? You still can render sacrifices of praise and thanksgiving. You still can serve God with your lips and thoughts of gratitude. You still can exalt Him in your spirit and in your heart. You still can praise Him with the light that is in your eyes.

What shall I render to God? I shall give Him the most important gifts—my heart, mind and soul.

REFLECTIVE QUESTIONS

1. How can you still serve God?
2. How can you still praise God?
3. How can you still give glory to God?

PRAYER

Lord, I cannot thank you and praise you enough. I cannot beat you giving no matter how hard I try. But God, help me to show you how much I appreciate you. Help me to show you how much I love you. Grant me the grace to glorify you in every thought, word or movement of my being. Amen.

NOT DEAD YET

"Many a life has been injured by the constant expectation of death. It is life we have to deal with, not death. The best preparation for the night is to work diligently while the day lasts. The best preparation for death is life."
(George MacDonald, "Treasure of Courage and Confidence, p.300)

He was an elderly sickly man, but he never lost his sense of dignity and self-respect. He was meticulously dressed in pajamas, every hair on his balding head was in place. He had the newspapers from around the world in neat stacks on and around his bed. He spoke with a deep rich voice, "Come in young man, how are you?" I said, "I am fine but I am wondering about your health and welfare." "Oh, I couldn't be better" he said. I said, "I am glad to hear that…" He cut me off and said, "Well, what did you expect an old man wallowing in self-pity? I am not dead yet. I can still think, read, talk, analyze and criticize! "He sat up in his bed and began to preach to me.

"So many people come in here with pity in their eyes and sorrow in their voices. Some of them act as if I have one foot in the grave. Let me tell you something, I am not dead yet! I am more alive now then I have ever been. As long as I can breathe, as long as blood still flows through my vein, I will fight to stay alive. I will not surrender. I will live until the good Lord takes me." I stood there and all I could say was "Amen".

REFLECTIVE QUESTIONS

1. Do you feel as if you have one foot in the grave?
2. Do you feel as if you are more dead than alive?
3. What kind of attitude changes do you need to reflect a vibrant, living spirit?
4. What could you do to feel more *alive*?
5. What are some of the things you still can do to enjoy life?
6. What do you think God wants you to do?

PRAYER

Lord of Life, I thank you for life. I praise you for every second of every day. Please help me not to take my life for granted. Help me to enjoy every aspect of my life. Amen.

THE BEST IS YET TO COME

"Grow old along with me!
The best is yet to be,
The last of life, for which the first was made;
Our times are in His hand who saith,
    "A whole I planned,
Youth shows but half; trust God: See all, nor be afraid" **Robert Browning**

The best is yet to come! The future looks bright and beautiful. There is nothing but peace, joy and righteousness ahead of you. You have nothing to be afraid of or worried about. The best is yet to come. Do you believe that? Do you feel good about your future?

Often, we are fearful of the future. We see nothing but doom and gloom on the horizons. Sometimes we get sad and depressed when we think about the future. We are saddened because we think our best days are behind us and our worse days are before us. All we see is sickness, pain and death.

We must remember that beyond sickness, pain and death is life, peace and joy, we must never forget that God is in our past, present and future. Since God is in your present, He will give you the grace to get through your future. He will lead you to a bright, beautiful and bountiful future. One day heaven will be your home and there will be no pain, suffering or death. You will walk in paradise with God. The best is yet to come!

REFLECTIVE QUESTIONS

1. How do you feel about the future?
2. What do you think that Heaven will be like?
3. What are you looking forward to?

PRAYER

O Lord, I thank you for my past, present and future. You have always been good to me. You have always blessed me. You are such a wonderful, loving God who cares for me. I know my future looks good. I know that Heaven awaits me. So, I look forward to the day when I will be with you. I look forward to the day without sadness, sickness or disease. A life without hospitals, doctors and medication awaits us. I can't wait to be with you and live with joy, love and laughter. Amen.

THINK ON THESE THINGS

"Finally, brethren, whatsoever things are true, whatsoever things are honest, whatsoever things are just, whatsoever things are pure, whatsoever things are lovely, whatsoever things are of good report; if there be any virtue and if there be any praise, think on these things." (Philippians 4:8)

What are you thinking about? The doctor's diagnosis? The deadly disease ravishing your body? Are you filled with worry, doubt, fear and despair? Are you thinking about the welfare of your loved ones? Are you thinking about the death and dying? It is understandable and rational to think on those things that impact on your life. The question is, are you thinking about <u>all</u> those things? Are you thinking about the positive as well as the negative? Are you focusing more on your sorrow and not your joys?

You have the power to choose to think positive, joyful and peaceful thoughts. You can discipline your mind to think on those things which are true, pure, and lovely. There are many things that can fit these adjectives, but, there is one who fulfills all these terms. God is true, just, pure and lovely. Think about the fact that God is true. His son Jesus Christ is the way, the truth and the life. He is the essence of that which is honest, truthful and moral. Our God is just. God's sense of justice is best seen in the redemptive suffering of his son Jesus Christ. Jesus Christ was just and he died for the unjust. Think about it. Our God is pure. There is nothing about him that is evil, wicked or sinful. It is only through his Holiness that we are holy. Think about the fact that your holiness is not based on your religiosity but on your relationship with Christ. Finally, our God is lovely. God is love. Think about the fact that God so loved you that he sacrificed Jesus Christ on the cross for your salvation. There is no greater love than knowing that God loves you. His love is unconditional and unlimited. His love is what will preserve your soul until it is united with Him in eternity. You have a choice in life. You can choose to think on life's negatives or Gods positives. Thinking about God will give you peace of mind and bountiful blessings.

REFLECTIVE QUESTIONS

1. How does thinking about the truth of God help you?
2. How does thinking about the purity of God help you?
3. How does thinking about the love of God help you?
4. How does thinking about the justice of God help you?

PRAYER

Oh God, I praise you, you and you alone are pure, just, lovely and true. Help me to think about you, Help, me to meditate on you. Give me positive prayers and uplifting thoughts that I may experience your peace and joy. Amen.

YOUR GREATEST GLORY

"Our greatest glory is not in never falling, but in rising every time we fall."- Oliver Goldsmith

You are never ultimately defeated until you have totally surrendered to your circumstances. If you still believe in God and his ability to care for you, you are not defeated. If you can wake up in the morning and find joy in the simplest things of life, you are not defeated. You are not defeated because you are sick, immobile, depressed or dying. You are not defeated because you can no longer do the things you used to do. You are not defeated because you not cured. Your victory is in the fact that your spirit is unbroken, your glory is that you are in the presence of God! Your power is in the fact that the Lord is your light and your salvation. You are triumphant simply because the Lord fights your battles. You are more than conqueror because of your divine attitude that refuses to quit, give up or give out. You may have your bad days, and you may get down every now and then. But you will never stay down simply because there is something within you that will not be suppressed, held back, rejected or defeated. It matters not how weak your body, how broken your heart, how desperate the circumstances, there is greatness in you, and you will rise every time you fall!

REFLECTIVE QUESTIONS

1. How do you feel and why?
2. Can you have a victorious attitude even when life circumstances can make you feel defeated?
3. How does faith in God give you the victory?
4. Share ways in which you have made a comeback from adversity.

<u>PRAYER</u>

Oh Lord, I thank you for the victory! I thank you for fighting my battles. I know that if you are with me. I can overcome what I face. I thank you for the victory. Amen.

EARLY DEATH

"Heaven gives its favorites-early death." – Lord Byron

When death comes early and unexpectedly, it can destabilize us, we become shocked, hurt, broken and bitterly disappointed. We can feel frustrated and angry at the injustice of it all. It does not seem fair that the good die so young. Why is it that the innocent die early, the young perish before their prime and the elderly die with dreams unfulfilled? Death comes much too early. Psychologically, we may not be prepared but, spiritually we are. For if we were not, God would not have taken us home to be with him. We must realize the fact that our time frame is different from heaven's time frame. Our life plan is grossly different from God's plan. Early death is a sign of God's grace and love. A love that will not wait for our time plan. A love that grants grace for the living and external reward for that dying. We are stronger than we think we are, we are more blessed than we realize. Early death is not a sign of divine injustice but, it is a symbol of divine grace and your unconscious spiritual maturity. Your soul is more ready than you realize. Moreover, God knows you and the entire situation better than you do. So even though you may feel angry, shocked and disappointed, you must trust that God has your best interest in mind. Trust that God will get you and your loved ones through this and you will be eternally blessed.

REFLECTIVE QUESTIONS

1. How do you really feel about early death?
2. Are you willing to trust Gods' time frame and plan rather than your own?
3. What are the possible blessings of premature death?

PRAYER

O God I trust you. I believe in you. I love you. But I do not understand why you do the things that you do. Your will is a mystery to me. Your divine plan is incomprehensible. I cannot fathom why this is happening to me. But I believe that you love me and will take care of me. I have faith that all things work together for good for those who love you and are called according to your purpose. I will trust in you with all my heart and not lean to my own understanding. Therefore, despite all my questions and doubts I thank you and praise you. Even with my bitter disappointment, I will magnify and glorify your name. Your goodness and mercy are with me. AMEN

YOU ARE GETTING BETTER

"Death is the opening of a more subtle life. In the flower, it sets free the perfume; in the chrysalis, the butterfly; in man, the soul." - **Juliette Adam**

Are you getting better? The answer to that question depends on your perspective. If you answer the question from a medical, physiological, psychological, financial, or social perspective, you might answer in the negative. You may feel as if you are getting worse, not better. You may be going through physical deterioration, psychological depression, financial deprivation, and social alienation. The death and dying process has a way of making you feel miserable and hopeless.

If you begin to see that physical deterioration ultimately leads to spiritual liberation, then you will see your status in a different perspective. You are getting better when you understand that the dying process can lead to spiritual renewal and redemption. You are getting better when you understand that death leads to eternal life and communion with God. You are getting better when you realize that all your pain and sorrow will give way to eternal joy and peace. Do not focus on the fact that you are dying but, remember that your soul is developing and being prepared for eternal life. You are not getting worse, every day your soul gets holier and holier.

One day your soul will break forth from its cocoon and you will fly away to glory. One day you will be resurrected as a new being, better, beautiful and radiating the love God. Each day brings you closer and closer to be a better you. Every day your soul gets better and better.

REFLECTIVE QUESTIONS

1. Do you speak positive thoughts to yourself?

2. What can you do to develop spiritually, emotionally and socially?

3. How is God making your soul better?

PRAYER

God of Grace and Glory I thank you for the spiritual growth I have in you. I praise you for the grace that transforms my soul into your Divine image. It is because of your grace that I am becoming a new creature every day. Every day I get better and better. Every day I get closer and closer to you. Every day I am becoming more and more like you. Thank you, Lord. Amen

IT'S TIME TO LIVE

"Oh God, to have reached the point of death without ever having lived at all." - Thoreau

There are some people who have never learned how to live life to the fullest, they have not discovered how to get the most out of life. Consequently, they lived mediocre lives and a bored existence. Rarely, do they let themselves get excited or moved by anyone or anything. They have never set any goals or pursued any daring dreams. Consequently, they are average and satisfied with the status quo. They are not fully committed to anyone or anything. They have wasted their God given abilities and opportunities.

If this has been your life, and you are approaching the grave, it is time for a change. It is time to live and enjoy your life and begin to do the things that you always wanted to do. You might not be able to do a lot of things, but, whatever you can do, you need to do it. It is time to live your life. It is time to live and express yourself. Tell people your joys and sorrows. It is not time to die. It is time to live. It is time to live your life to the fullest. If you have a dream fulfill it. If you can correct a past situation rectify it. If you still have love in your heart show it. If you still have a goal, pursue it. If you still want something, pursue it. If you still have a testimony, share it. If you want to get right with God, do it. Whatever you need to do, do it! You are not dead yet. You still have time. Go ahead and live your life!

REFLECTIVE QUESTIONS

1. What do you want to do with the rest of your life?
2. What brings you joy or passion in life?
3. What "unfinished business" do you have to accomplish?
4. What are some things you still want and can do?
5. Who do you need to talk to before you die?

PRAYER

O God you are the Resurrection and the Life. You are the one who grants me life and opportunities in life. Help me not to waste time. Grant me the grace to use my time wisely and to your glory. Amen.

YOU ARE AN ARTIST

"You have your brush, you have your colors, and you paint paradise, then in you go." – Nikos Kazantzakis

You are an artist and you have the option to paint your self-portrait on life's canvas. It is up to you to use your creative imagination and courage of your convictions to live out the end of your life. Painting the picture of your life is up to you, no one or nothing can paint your portrait but you. Only you can express who you are. So, your life maybe as colorful as you want it to be. You must choose the kind of colors which are your feelings, thoughts, ideas or dreams that expresses who you are. Paint the portrait of your life and enjoy its view. If you do not like the way you look, repaint it again. Remember you have the brush; the colors and you are the artist.

REFLECTIVE QUESTIONS

1. What are some of the creative things that you could do or say that would make your life better?
2. How could you affirm the life that you have?
3. What else could you do to enjoy your life?

PRAYERS:

Almighty God, I thank you for life. I pray that you will grant me the grace to experience the abundant life. Enable me to live a life of love, joy, peace and righteousness. Lord, I thank you that you have given me the choices to create a life that is beautiful and glorious. Amen

EXCESS BAGGAGE

"Excess baggage is all these things that we can see about ourselves that keep getting in our way. It could be a flaw, a weakness, a failing, a fear, an ideology, an old passion, bad habits or pieces of your past that impede you from living a pleasurable, productive life." – Dr. Judith Sills

What is your excess baggage?

What are the negative feelings, self-destructive behaviors, bad attitudes or regrets that keep you from going forward?

Is it a relationship that has been ruined and makes you feel bitter? Is it the fear of death that has paralyzed you? Is it guilt and regret of the past?

Is it your loss of control and you feel frustrated and upset? Whatever your excess baggage is, give it to God. Allow God to carry your self-imposed burdens. He states, "Come unto me all you who are burdened and heave laden and I will give you rest." Share your feelings to Jesus Christ and He will take all your excess baggage from you. He will alleviate you of all your negative thoughts, feelings and habits. He will give you a life of joy, peace and love. He will lighten your load. He will give your soul rest and peace. So, if you feel overwhelmed give your burdens to Jesus. Tell him all about your troubles, worries and feelings. He will soothe and comfort your weary soul.

REFLECTIVE QUESTIONS

1. What kind of excess baggage do you have?
2. What negative thoughts, feelings or circumstances bring your spirit down?
3. Have you prayed to God and shared all your excess baggage? Why or why not?
4. How do you feel carrying all your burdens?

5. What could you do to assist someone's excess baggage?
6. Are you feeling overwhelmed with thought of dying?

PRAYER

Almighty God, I give you my excess baggage. I give you all my fears, frustrations, anger, sadness, guilt, jealousy, bitterness, stress, and negativity. I cannot bear these burdens any longer. Allow me to experience your peace, your love and your joy. Amen

GODS DECISION

"If not me then who? If not now, then when?" – Ancient Jewish teaching

We all must die sometime. No one can escape death. It does not matter how much money you have; what your educational level; what your genetic makeup; what kind of social background; what the status of your health is or how spiritual you are, you will die.

Our being, no matter how religious, healthy and successful, cannot stop death from taking us. You may ask why me?! Why does death want me? Why not take someone else? God has chosen you not for death but for eternal life. A life without pain, suffering and heartache. A life with God and a home in glory. You may still ask," why now of all times? There is still a lot I want to do. Why not take me later? This is a bad time for my fragile family!"

God knows the best times to take us home. He knows what the best day and time for would be all concerned. God knows all those persons who will be affected by your death. He knows all the things that they will go through. God knows the situation and your loved ones a lot better than you. You must trust in the omniscience of God. You must believe that God knows the best time. His time frame is different from your time frame because He knows what's best for all concerned. So trust that whatever God does for you, He does out of love, wisdom and grace. God's decision is always the right decision.

REFLECTIVE QUESTIONS

1. How do you feel about dying at this time in your life?
2. Why do you think that God is taking you to Heaven?
3. What are the possible positive consequences to your early death?

PRAYER

Almighty God I trust you. I trust that you know the best day and time for my death. I trust that you will take care of my family and friends when I am dead. I trust that you know what is best for all of us because you love us so much. Amen.

PASS THE TORCH

"Those having torches will pass them on to others."- Plato

It is time to pass the torch. It is time to share all your insights, knowledge, resources, wisdom, and love to others. You have a legacy that needs to be shared with your loved ones. It is the story of your victories and defeats. It is the songs of your soul. It is a message of hope to those who are living in despair. You have something to say and God has blessed you with someone to say it to. Pass the torch which is the flame of your spirit. Tell someone the stories of your life. Share with them all the struggles that you have gone through. Share not only your victories, share your defeats. They can learn from your experiences. Witness to them what the Lord has done for you. Your witness will fortify their faith and give them courage. Pass the torch, the fire in your soul and you will live on in others.

REFLECTIVE QUESTIONS

1. What is your legacy?
2. Who can you share your legacy with?
3. How do you want to be remembered?
4. Share some of your stories of success and failure.
5. Share your testimony about the grace of God on your life.

PRAYER

O Lord, you have given me the torch that has burned brightly. You have given me a story to tell, a song to sing, a sermon to preach, a lesson to teach, a wisdom to impart. Help me not to be selfish, shy, or too insecure to share my gifts and graces. Grant me the faith to pass this torch that others may continue the race. Amen.

POWER OVER PAIN

"No one can hurt you without your consent." – Eleanor Roosevelt

You have power over pain, suffering, disease, even death. Nothing or no one can destroy your spirit unless you allow it. The pain that you feel does not have to dampen your courage. Despite your suffering, you can respond with joy and fearlessness. The sickness that you are enduring cannot touch your soul. It is impervious to the attacks of sickness and pain. It can withstand anything that comes at you. God's presence permeates your soul and makes it indestructible. His spirit is like a force field which cannot be destroyed. Therefore, you do not have to succumb to any obstacles or problems. You have power over your body and your circumstances. You have power to choose what kind of attitude that you will have. You do not have to succumb to your fears, doubts, anger and despair. You can choose to have a positive attitude and a victorious spirit. No one or nothing can hurt you unless you let them.

REFLECTIVE QUESTIONS

1. What do you feel weak or powerless about?
2. What kind of attitude do you have and are you willing to change?
3. How does God give you power over your limited and debilitating circumstances?

PRAYER

O Lord I am weak, powerless and frail without you. Without you, I am defeated but with you I am victorious. You give me victory over sickness, suffering, sin, Satan and death. I have the victory, the power, and the glory because I have you and you have me. Amen.

THINK OF YOURSELF DIFFERENTLY

"As a man thinketh in his heart so shall he be." (Proverbs 27:3)

Who are you and what are you becoming? Do you like what you see in the mirror? What do you think about yourself? These can be very challenging questions for those who may be terminally ill and deteriorating physically. Often, we feel depressed because sickness has ravaged our body. Our overall appearance has deteriorated. Our physical abilities are limited. We may think of ourselves as ugly, repulsive and worthless. We notice that others look at us differently. We become self-conscious and think negatively of ourselves.

We are much, much more than what we appear to be. We must think of ourselves as God's son or daughter. Our appearance has nothing to do with our inestimable worth and divine dignity. You are a child of God. You are a royal priesthood. A citizen of the Kingdom of God. You are special. You are unique. There is no one else like you and there will never ever will be. You need to think of yourself as God thinks of you. Be proud of who you were, who you are, and who you are becoming. You were a child of God in the past, in the present and in the future. Do not think of yourself as others may think of you, but, think of yourself as God thinks of you. You are His child. You are fearfully and wonderfully made. Look into the mirror and tell yourself how wonderful and great you are. Give God praise for who you are and what you are becoming.

REFLECTIVE QUESTIONS

1. What do you think of yourself and why?
2. How do you think others think of you?
3. What do you think God thinks of you?
4. Why do we care more about our physical appearance instead of the status of our souls?

PRAYER

Almighty Father, I thank you for thinking of me as your child. Help me to see myself as you see me. Open my eyes that I can see the beauty of your holiness within my soul. Allow me to see your presence, your glory, and your love. Amen.

WHERE WILL YOU GO?

"The mind is its own place, and in itself can make a heaven of hell, a hell of heaven." – John Milton

Where will you go? Your thoughts have enormous power to alter your feelings, attitude, and your perspective on life. In a sense, your thoughts can determine where you will go. One can either ascend to heights of joy or rapture with heavenly thoughts. Or, one could descend to the depths of despair with negative thoughts. It is not your physical environment that is so critical to your emotional wellbeing, but it is your mental status. Your mind can transform a lonely, depressing nursing home into a haven of happiness. It can create a hospital of sickness and suffering to a Disney Land of delight and joy. Your bed of affliction can be transformed into a comfort zone of God's grace and glory! Your wheelchair does not have to be perceived as a metal prison, it can be a professorial chair from which you can impart wisdom and knowledge. Death does not have to be perceived as the end of life, it can be a new beginning. It's not your external condition or circumstances that matters. It is your internal condition that counts. How you feel and what you think of things is what makes the difference in your life. So, the question is not how I can escape my circumstances, or how can I leave this dreaded place? The question is how can I think of my circumstances differently? How can I see the positive side in all of this? The difference is all in your heart and mind.

REFLECTIVE QUESTIONS

1. What do you think about where you live?
2. What kind of thoughts do you have about yourself?
3. How can you think of your life in more positive terms?

PRAYER

O Lord, I thank and praise you for the beauty and grace I see throughout all your creation. Your presence can be seen and experience even in the worst conditions. Your love can be felt even when no one seems to care. I experience your joy and peace even during chaos and confusion. I thank you for making me Heavenly minded in this earthly setting. Amen.

MASTER YOUR PASSION

"The happiness of man in this life does not consist in the absence but in the mastery of his passion."- Alfred Tennyson

As human beings, we are all vulnerable to a kaleidoscope of feelings and thoughts. It is in our nature to feel sad, angry, guilty, joy, frustrated, lonely and hopeless. These and other feelings can dominate our consciousness if we allow them to, however, we have the power to choose what feeling we will let control us. Our feelings do not master us, we master them. We can choose happiness, joy and peace. It is up to you. You don't have to allow feelings of brokenness to steal your joy. Your joy can stand free to express itself while other feelings are chained. You can allow those other negative feelings to express themselves, but they do not have to dictate your consciousness.

You can master your feelings. You can choose to feel good about your circumstances. When people ask you how you feel, tell them that you feel good! Tell them that God is good anyhow! Share your positive thoughts and feelings. Refuse to let sadness and despair overwhelm you. Remember you oversee the way you feel and nothing and no one can change that unless you let them.

REFLECTIVE QUESTIONS

1. What are you feeling right now?
2. What are some positive things that are happening in your life?
3. What could you say or do to feel good about yourself?

PRAYER

Almighty God I thank you for making me feel good despite my circumstances. Thank you for the joy and peace I have in you. Help me to choose to think positively. Amen.

MEDICINE OF MERRIMENT

"A laugh is just like music, it lingers in the heart, and where its melody is heard, ills of life depart." - Sanders

I walked into the hospital room to visit a friend of mine who was dying of a terminal disease. She was getting ready to eat breakfast and the nurse was present. The young nurse hovered over her and began to take her vital signs. She took her blood pressure, listened to her heart beat and did other medical procedures. Her family was sitting in the room and looked tired and weary. The nurse was wearing a button with a picture on it and my sick friend asked the nurse "Is that a picture of your boyfriend?" The nurse grinned and said, "Oh, no, it is my best friend though." My friend said, "It is too bad, he's good looking. I wonder if he will date me." The family and I looked at the picture pinned to the nurse's lapel and we all started to laugh. It was a picture of a dog! My sick friend had brought joy and laughter into a room of gloom. She revealed that sickness and death cannot take your joy away. You can still smile. You still can laugh. Her sense of humor was medicine for our soul.

REFLECTIVE QUESTIONS

1. What is humorous or joyful about your situation?
2. What makes you smile or laugh?

PRAYER

Thank you, God, for putting joy in my heart, a smile on my face and praise on my lips. You make life worth living. You give me something to smile about. Help me to see the humor in life. Thank you for the joy and the laughter you bring to my life. Amen.

REJOICE IN REALITY

Happiness is the mental state of contentment which comes from successful adoptions to the world as it really is. It comes from being useful, of contributing to the welfare and happiness of others.

There are many people who futilely attempt to deny reality. They are afraid of the truth and will do everything in their power to refute, destroy, or deny it. Some would rather live a lie than be told the truth. We assume that ignorance is bliss and awareness produce anguish. We find it very difficult to accept the fact that we are going to die. Or that our loved ones will no longer be with us. Consequently, we will try to deny death in our actions, words or feelings. The result is living a fantasy that will eventually shatter your foundation. It will leave you disillusioned and desperate.

Joy can be found in harsh reality. Just as a plant rises from a concrete sidewalk, so can our joy emerge from the cold, hard facts? Once you have accepted and embraced death, it liberates you from fear, frustration and sadness. Death does not destroy joy. It is fear of death that can rob us of our joy. Accepting life as it really is can be liberating. It frees us from the illusions of "medical miracles" and unrealistic prayers. We no longer must fool ourselves thinking that we are "in recovery" and "things are getting better." The truth of the matter is that we are not going to get physically better and we are dying. Once you have accepted that fact then you can begin to appreciate the miracle of the moment. There is a sense of inner peace and even joy found in learning to enjoy life now and not in the distant future. Happiness is not just in heaven, it's in you. You can experience some of the peace of Heaven in this life. In this life with all its sickness and suffering God can give you the ability to deal with your harsh reality. God may not change your circumstances, but He will change you to meet the circumstances. He will give you comfort during your affliction and holy strength for your physical weakness.

God will give you the faith and courage to face death and still praise Him. Whatever your reality is you can still rejoice in it.

REFLECTIVE QUESTIONS

1. Have you prayed to God to have him give you the faith to confront death?
2. Why or why not?
3. Have you accepted the fact that you are dying? Why or why not?
4. Can you accept that death is a miracle?

PRAYER

God, I thank you for the life I have right here and now. I know that I am dying and I accept that. In my acceptance give me peace of mind and happiness in my heart. Amen.

BITTER CUP

"He went away again the second time and prayed, 'O My Father, if this cup may not pass away from me, except I drink it, thy will be done." *(Matthew 26:42)*

Jesus struggled all night long about his impending death. He knew that the Scribes and Pharisees were conspiring get him and persecute him. He knew that the mighty Roman Empire would arrest him, interrogate him, and crucify him. The powers that be felt threatened by Jesus' growing grass roots appeal and preaching the Kingdom of God which was a direct attack on the status quo. Death was imminent for Jesus and it is only a matter of time before he would meet his end.

Naturally Jesus felt overwhelmed with grief and despair. The human side of Jesus wanted to live and be with his disciples, friends and family. He wanted to continue to love and serve God and humanity. The thought of dying and being apart from his loved ones broke his heart and crushed his spirit. He felt weary and sad. He needed time alone with his disciples to pray and renew his spirit.

The Garden of Gethsemane offered Jesus and his disciples the peace and quiet that they needed. Unfortunately, the disciples were so weary that they fell asleep praying for him, still Jesus continued to pray to God asking for "this cup to be taken away...." (Matthew 26:42) Jesus did not want to drink the bitter cup of suffering and death. Jesus did not want to die. He did not want to suffer. He wanted to live and so he begged God to deliver him He asked God to let the bitter cup of pain and death to pass him by.

You may be at the point in your life when you are confronted with the bitter cup. The bitter cup may mean sickness, suffering and disease. It could be realizing that you are going to die and there is nothing you can do about it. The bitter cup could mean rejection, loneliness and alienation. It may mean unrequited love and the heart break of feeling ignored and uncared for. The bitter cup could be unanswered prayer. It is dying prematurely with your work unfinished and your dreams unfulfilled. The bitter cup could be watching your loved one slowly die. Its horrifying spectacle of watching your beloved deteriorate before your very eyes. In one way or another we all drink the bitter cup. Even Jesus the Son of God had to drink from the bitter cup.

Jesus prayed for the bitter cup to pass but it remained. He wanted an escape from his impending suffering and death, but there was no escape from the cross. God still allowed him to be crucified and die a painful death. God answered Jesus prayer but not in the way he requested. Unfortunately, Jesus had to drink every painful drop of the bitter cup. He had to pray until he totally submitted to the will of God. Once Jesus prayed, "your will be done" he surrendered himself to the inevitability of his death. Once Jesus said, "Thy will be done" God gave Jesus the grace to accept the unacceptable. God enabled Jesus to accept His will and all its difficulties.

Once you say in your heart, "Thy will be done" God will give you the grace to drink from the bitter cup. You will be able to cope with all your pain, agony and loss. God will give you the courage to face death and still have peace. You will have peace knowing that God is with you and nothing can separate you from His love. His love will preserve and protect your soul from death and its diabolical devices. A loving relationship with God can overcome the sting of death. His love for you will give you grace to die with dignity and the divinity to experience eternal life. You have nothing to fear or get upset by drinking from the bitter cup. It will inevitably make you stronger in your faith and love. As T.B. Matson once said" bitter experiences are not made to make us bitter Christians but better Christians." So, let us drink from the bitter cup knowing that we do not drink alone. God is with us through every bitter experience in life.

PRAYER

Almighty God, it is my prayer that you do a miracle in my life. I pray that you would heal me and restore to me my life in its fullness. I don't want to die. I want to live. Nor do I want my loved one to die. So, it is my sincere prayer that you allow me to live if I can. But if it is your will for me to die give me the grace to accept it Help me to discover the peace that comes with accepting your will. Grant me to have faith to see that death is a miracle for it means experiencing your love for all eternity. Help me to say thy will be done. Amen

REFLECTIVE QUESTIONS

1. What is your bitter cup?
2. How are you presently coping with it?
3. Have you prayed to God about your bitter cup?
4. How can this difficult experience bring you closer to God?
5. How can this harsh experience bring you closer to others?
6. What do you think the will of God is in your life?
7. Have you accepted the will of God in your life?
8. The will of God may mean pain and suffering. Can you accept that harsh reality? Why or why not?

WELL DONE

"Well done thou good and faithful servant. Thou hast been faithful over a few things, I will make thee a ruler over many things. Enter thou into the joy of the Lord." (Matthew 25:21)

He was an eighty-year-old man slumped over sleeping in his wheelchair. His hair was grey, his clothes were wrinkled, and his body appeared weak and frail. I almost hadn't recognized him. This man was a prominent pastor of an urban church and a powerful, influential leader in the community. The cancer had totally deteriorated him, and his dementia had reduced his capacity to understand simple sentences. After I had gotten over my initial shock, I tried to awaken him with words of comfort. He barely moved and hardly spoke. Then I began to recite all his accomplishments and service to God and the church. He still didn't move or speak. Then I told him that when he dies God will say to him, "Well done thou good and faithful servant. You have been faithful over a few things, I will make you a ruler over many things. Enter into the joy of the Lord." Suddenly, he woke up and sat up in his wheelchair. He stopped slouching and sat erect with his shoulders back and his head up. It was as if someone had given him a shot of adrenalin. He seemed alive, animated and energized. His whole demeanor had changed. There was an effervescent spirit about him. It seemed as if hearing those powerful words, "Well done thou good and faithful servant "had resurrected his spirit. It seemed as if those words had touched him to the core of his being and reaffirmed his whole life. Those words reminded him that God loved him and would reward him for all his service and sacrifice. "Well done thou good and faithful servant." are the words that every child of God yearns to hear from their Heavenly Father. There is no greater compliment in all the world than those given by our Savior. It one thing for man to say something nice about you it's another thing for God to compliment your work. His judgment is fair and just. Moreover, God remembers every little sacrifice, service and acts of kindness.

You may never be fully appreciated or complimented in this life, but you will surely be rewarded in the next life. God will reward all his servants who have been faithful to him. He promises a crown of life, a robe of righteousness and a mansion in glory. These eternal riches and much more to those who have given their life to Him. All of these spiritual treasures will never compare to those powerful words from the Master himself," Well done thou good and faithful servant…Well done!

PRAYER

Almighty God, I thank you for allowing me the privilege to serve you. It is an honor to sacrifice, struggle and work on your behalf. I hope that your grace will look beyond all the times when I have not been so good and faithful. Please look beyond my unfaithfulness and see the faithfulness of your Son Jesus the Christ who resides in me. It is through Him and with Him that I will hear you say, Well done. Amen

REFLECTIVE QUESTIONS

1. What are some of the services that you have rendered in the church?
2. What are some of the services that you have rendered in the community?
3. What service or deed to humankind that are you most proud of?
4. What do you think God will say to you in Heaven? Why?
5. Are you pleased with your life? Why or why not?
6. What unfinished business do you still have to do?
7. Have asked God to forgive you of those things you have not completed or started?

8. Have you forgiven yourself of any unfinished business?
9. How do you define a "good and faithful servant"?
10. How do you think God defines a "good and faithful servant."?
11. Do you think that you will go to heaven? Why or why not?

VICTORY IS MINE

"But thanks be to God, which giveth us the victory through our Lord Jesus Christ." (I. Corinthians 15:57)

You have the victory. The fact that Jesus Christ has overcome Satan, sin, suffering, sickness and death on the cross guarantees you the victory. The victory is in the death, burial, and resurrection of Jesus Christ. It is in Him, through Him and with Him that you have the victory. Often, we measure victory by worldly superficial standards. The world determines victory by money, possessions, power, property and prestige. Some would say a disease that has gone into remission is victory or the cure for cancer is victory. A positive diagnosis from a doctor is said to be victory, however, there is another deeper, profound victory that is found in the spiritual realm. It is the victory of a soul that cannot be broken or saddened by sickness, suffering or death. It is a victory of a soul that has submitted to Jesus Christ as Lord and Savior. It is victory knowing that no matter what happens, God is always present. Never forget if you are in Christ you have the victory.

REFLECTIVE QUESTIONS

1. What does it mean to have the victory?
2. What kind of attitude should I have to reflect a victorious spirit?
3. What kind of behavior or attitude do I need to reveal victory in Christ?

PRAYER

Almighty God, you have rescued us from the jaws of death, defeat and despair. I praise you for your power, presence and deliverance. I thank you for the victory found in the resurrection of Jesus Christ. It is in His resurrected spirit that I claim the victory. Amen.

FORGIVE AND FORGET

"I, even I am He that blotted out thy transgressions for my own sake; and will not remember thy sins." (Isaiah 43:25)

Sometimes we find it very hard to forgive ourselves. We are painfully aware of our sins and shortcomings. We remember what we did or what we failed to do. We would like to forget but we are haunted by our transgressions. Moreover, there are others who will not let us forget what we have done. Maybe we have hurt them, and their wounds are still fresh and have not healed. They hurt so they make us hurt. We should apologize as soon as possible, yet we cannot forgive them until we forgive ourselves. We must never forget about the grace and mercy of God that forgives and forgets. You may not forgive yourself, but God does. You may put yourself down, but God never will. It is the nature of God to be loving, caring, understanding and forgiving. He forgives you of your sins and cast them into a sea of forgetfulness. He refuses to remember or record all your wrong doings. God is extremely merciful and quick to forgive us. All we need to do is pray and humbly confess our sins and shortcomings to Him. His grace is sufficient to compensate for all of our vices, weaknesses, addictions and failures. God can forgive you it's time for you to forgive yourself.

REFLECTIVE QUESTIONS

1. What are you feeling guilty about?
2. Do others make you feel guilty and why?
3. When will you forgive yourself?
4. Have you accepted the grace and mercy of our Lord who forgives us of all our sins?

PRAYER

God of Grace and God of Glory. I realize that I have sinned and fallen short of your glory. I confess all my past, present, and future sins and ask that you forgive them all. Please heal me of my guilt and shame. Let your blood wash me and cleanse me of all unrighteousness. Help me to understand that your grace and mercy is far greater than my guilt. Allow me to experience the warm embrace of your loving heart that I may accept myself. Amen.

BIRDS OF SORROW

"You cannot prevent the birds of sorrow from flying over your head, but you can prevent them from building nests in your hair."- Chinese Proverb

It is natural for you to feel sad and to cry sometimes, in fact if you did not grieve there maybe something seriously wrong with you. Tears are a natural part of the grieving process. Sorrow, despair and dejection are human emotions.

To prolong the feelings of sorrow and wallow in self-pity is to invite the birds of sorrow to build a nest on your soul. The birds of sorrow sing the blues and make you feel sorry for yourself. They constantly pick and eat away all the joy from your spirit. If you let them build a nest, they will produce more birds of sorrow, eventually they will dominate your entire being and eat all the fruit of the spirit from your branches. You will no longer be able to express joy, patience, long suffering, gentleness, self-control, kindness, love, and peace.

Do not let the birds of sorrow build a nest in your spirit. Begin to think positive thoughts. Count your blessing. Be thankful for all of life's little blessings and you will discover that the birds of sorrow will leave the nest on your soul.

REFLECTIVE QUESTIONS

1. Are the birds of sorrow building a nest in your soul?
2. Do you have a positive or a negative attitude?
3. What kind of positive thoughts can you have?
4. What are you thankful for?

PRAYER

Heavenly Father I thank you for all your blessings. I praise you for all the good that you have done and are doing for me. Forgive me when I have felt sorry for myself and became bitter and sad. Help me to focus on all of life's blessings rather than its burdens. Guide my thoughts that they may meditate on the prince of peace. Amen.

GOING HOME

"Let not your heart be troubled ye believe in God believe also in me. In my Father's house are many mansions. If it were not so I would have told you. I go to prepare a place for you and if I go to prepare a place for you I will come again and receive you unto myself that where I am there ye maybe also." (John 14:1-3)

The disciples of Jesus were troubled because they knew that their Lord was going to be persecuted. They knew it was only a matter of time before his enemies would destroy him. The disciples were not only afraid for Jesus they were afraid for themselves. They were fearful for their own lives. They were afraid of being persecuted. They were afraid of dying. Is there life after death? What will happen to them when they die? Will they end up dying on a cross and then buried in some obscure shallow grave? The disciples were fearful and troubled about their lives?

Jesus comforts his disciples by reminding them to believe in God and in himself. It is their belief in their relationship with God that will preserve them through all their ordeals. The disciples were comforted by the fact that God was with them and that a special place was prepared for them. Jesus promised his disciples a life beyond this life. He assures them that when they die, they will go to a heavenly home. A heavenly home where there are no Scribes and Pharisees to persecute them, Roman soldiers to crucify them, or death to destroy them. The disciples need not be troubled. They will be home with God.

It is the same with you. You need not be troubled by death. If you believe in God and his Son, He will care for you. You can be comforted in the fact that God is with you through all your struggles. Not only will God be with you in this life but also the next life. He promises you a heavenly home. A heavenly home where there is no sickness, suffering, disease or death. A heavenly home where God will wipe away all tears from your eyes, heal your broken heart and put joy bells in your soul. So, don't be afraid or troubled. You are going home!

PRAYER

Almighty God, I want to live and be with my family and friends. I really don't want to die. I'm afraid of dying. I don't know what the future holds for me. Give me the faith to realize that you are with me and together we can overcome my challenges. Give me the faith to see that I have a life beyond this life. A heavenly home with you and all my loved ones who have gone on before me. A heavenly home where there is nothing but peace, love and joy. A heavenly home where there is no evil, injustice or suffering. A heavenly home where we shall experience love and laughter and the indescribable holiness of your presence. I cannot wait to go home and be with you. For when I am at home with you, I have all that I ever wanted or needed. Amen

REFLECTION

1. Are you afraid of dying?
2. What troubles you about dying?
3. What do you think will happen to you when you die?
4. What do you think heaven will be like?
5. Do you believe that you are going to heaven? Why or why not?
6. What do you think God will say to you when you meet Him?
7. What do you need to do before you go to heaven?
8. Do you believe in the death burial and resurrection of Jesus Christ? Why or why not?

AUTUMN LEAVES

"Let life be beautiful like summer flowers and death like autumn leaves." - Tagore

You are an autumn leaf. You are colorful, beautiful and purposeful. The leaves must live for a period of time, but they also must fall. It is in their falling that their greater purpose is rendered. It is their task to reveal the tree, the source of their life. As an autumn leaf, you are called to reveal the tree or the wooden cross of Calvary. It is up to you to change, to get weak, fall and expose the source of your strength-Jesus Christ.

The death and dying process has a way of changing us. No matter how futile we try to cover up, conceal and deny death it inevitably changes us. There is nothing wrong with these changes. In fact, it is natural for human beings to get old, weak, ill and die. We must begin to see ourselves like the autumn leaf. Our physical and emotional changes are a good thing. We should accept them and allow nature to take its place. See yourself changing and becoming weaker and weaker. Know that you are becoming more and more beautiful, and one day your beauty will really shine as you fall and expose the Tree of Life.

<u>REFLECTIVE QUESTIONS</u>

1. In what ways have you physically changed and how do you feel about it?
2. In what ways have you changed emotionally and how do you feel about it?
3. How has the death and dying process changed you?
4. What are the positive aspects of your change?

PRAYER

O God of life who gives us life. We see your life in every season of life. In good and in bad times, in times of health and sickness, in times of strength and weakness you are forever with us. Help me to see and appreciate you during all of life's changes Help me to testify of your goodness and grace through every transition. Grant me the grace to fall, to let go, to die with the beauty of your holiness upon my face. Amen.

SHINING STAR

"Night brings out stars as sorrows show us truths." – Philip James Bailey

There are shining stars brightly in the midnight of your mourning. They shine for all who have the eyes to see it. There is the star of hope that reminds you of the fact that death is not the end of life but its glorious beginning. Can't you see it? It shines when you remember that death is only a doorway into eternal life. There is a star of love that shines. It shines allowing you see the beauty that comes with companionship. Look into the eyes of your loved one and you can see love. Love they have for you and for others. Finally, there is the star of peace. The more you meditate on peaceful thoughts the more you can see it. The star of peace gives you peace. It maybe night time in your life but rejoice, your stars shine bright in the night.

REFLECTIVE QUESTIONS

1. What are the stars in your night life that shine brightly?
2. What truth or insights have you learned about the night of your sorrows?

PRAYER

God of light and God of life I seek your light in the darkness of my despair. I search for your light in the midnight of my morning. Open my eyes that I may see the Bright Morning Star of your presence in my life and in my circumstances. Let me see your star shine in me and in others that I may glorify your name. Amen.

PARADISE IN THE MIDST OF PAIN

"And he said unto Jesus, "Lord, remember me when thou comest into thy Kingdom. And Jesus said unto him, "Verily, I say unto thee, today shalt thou be with me in Paradise." (Luke 23:42, 43)

Blood, sweat and tears pouring down his battered body. Excruciating pain surging through every ounce of his being. His close friends and family had deserted him. Even a thief on cross had vilified and denounced him. Despite his enormous emotional physical pain, Jesus uttered, "Today thou shalt be with me in paradise." Jesus had paradise during pain. He was able to proclaim victory in the throes of defeat. He could have complained, cried out even given up, but his indomitable spirit transcended his pain and glimpsed at paradise.

Paradise is not just an eschatological hope, a theological abstraction. It is a state of mind in which every believer can arrive. Paradise is a matter of divine perspective.

Paradise is the inner peace that comes with knowing of God's constant love. It is when the soul communes with the lord. No matter what you are feeling, you can experience paradise. Paradise is being one with God enveloped in his love. It is a deeply intimate, personal relationship with his son Jesus Christ. If you know Jesus as your personal Lord and savior, you have paradise. Talking to God and listening to him is paradise. No matter what you are going thru hear our Lord say to you, "You will be with me in Paradise."

REFLECTIVE QUESTIONS

1. What do you think paradise will be?
2. How can you have a "paradise perspective?"

PRAYER

Lord, I am in so much pain and despair. This cross that I am bearing is unbearable. Speak to me of your paradise. Allow me to experience the power of your presence that will enable me to transcend my circumstances. Grant me paradise of being with you now and forever more. Amen.

POWER FOR THE POWERLESS

"He giveth power to the faint, and them that have no might He increaseth strength. Even the youths shall faint and be weary and the young men shall utterly fall, but they that wait upon the Lord shall renew their strength; they shall mount up with wings like eagles, they shall run and not be weary, they shall walk and not faint." (Isaiah 40:29–31)

Are you feeling tired, weak, drained by this entire experience? Do you feel as if your prayers are in vain and God is not answering them? Do you feel irritable, perturbed and anxious? Do you feel as if you cannot go on anymore?

If you feel this way, then it is time to wait on the Lord. It is time to stop relying on your own strength and begin to rely on the Lord. He is power for the powerless. Once we accept the fact that we cannot do it alone, that we need help, God grants us the power to go on. You must acknowledge your weakness and let God give you the grace to go on. Admit it to yourself and to God that it is impossible for you to cope with illness and terminality. Confess your weakness and lack of faith. Once you acknowledge your powerlessness God will give you power. The more you empty yourself of self-sufficiency the more God will fill you with is grace and glory.

REFLECTIVE QUESTIONS

1. Do you feel powerless and weak?
2. Have you admitted to yourself that you can't cope with all this by yourself?
3. Have you asked God for more strength?

PRAYER

Lord, I need you. I need your power. I need your strength. I need your perseverance. I cannot do it alone. Please give me the power I need to live this life, to die in dignity and to be raised in glory. AMEN

IT WILL MAKE YOU NOT BREAK YOU

"Many men owe the grandeur of their lives to their tremendous difficulties." –
Charles Spurgeon

Life's difficulties will make you not break you. Sickness, suffering, even the dying process has the potential to fortify your faith, build your character, strengthen your soul and sensitized your heart. Your body may decay but your inner spirit is renewed, replenished, revamped, restored and revitalized.

Many ordinary people have become extraordinary because of trials and tribulations. Great preachers, politician's athletes, entertainers, artist, pioneers, achievers and leaders have been developed by their adversities. Martin Luther King, Jr., Maya Angelo, Abraham Lincoln, Harriet Tubman, Sojourner Truth, Nelson Mandela, Oprah Winfrey and many others have been hammered on the anvil of greatness. The one thing that great leaders and achievers have in common is that they their hardships have helped to develop their character and skills.

Therefore, know that whatever you are experiencing cannot break your spirit unless you let it. You can withstand anything that comes your way. Keep in mind that God will give you strength to not only endure but to grow through it and despite it. Moreover, you will be a stronger wiser and holier as a result of it.

REFLECTIVE QUESTIONS

1. How can this experience help you to grow?
2. can this experience help others to grow?
3. In what ways have you developed and become a better person?

PRAYER

O God I thank you and praise you for your grace that empowers me to go through this difficult experience. I am grateful that as a result of this burden I am becoming better, stronger each day. I know that it is your will that this painful process is for my ultimate good. Amen.

THE MIND IS A BATTLEFIELD

"Do you know that your thoughts rule your life, be they pure or impure? As you think-so you are, And you make or you mar your success in the world By your thoughts" - Anonymous

What are you thinking about? Are you thinking about death? Are you worried about your loved ones? Are you feeling anxious about the illness and what tomorrow will bring? Is your mind filled with negative thoughts, ideas and feelings? Is it becoming hard for you to see the positive side of life? If you have answered affirmative to any of these questions, understand that your mind is at war. Positive thoughts are at war with negative thoughts. This war of thoughts could go either way. You must choose to fight against fear, frustrations, negativity and morbidity that accompanies the death and dying process. You can win this war by remembering your secret weapon-God. Let thoughts of God's presence permeate your thinking. God will lead you in the battlefield of your mind. He will help you to think positive thoughts of things that are true, just, pure and lovely. You can win this battle, but you must fight with the weapons God gives you. Whenever you think of something that is painful remember a blessing be thankful. Allow the spirit of gratitude and joy to defeat the armies of darkness and despair. Fight those negative thoughts with positive thoughts. Defeat those bad beliefs with good thoughts. Use God's word, the sword of the spirit to kill every depressing thought and feeling. You can win this battle if you remember to let the Lord fight your battle.

REFLECTIVE QUESTIONS

1. What are some of the negative thoughts that you have?
2. What are some of the positive thoughts that you could use to fight the negative ones?
3. What scriptures are comforting and encouraging to you?
4. What are some blessings that you are thankful for?

PRAYER

Oh Lord I pray that you will fight my battle. Defeat every evil thought, feeling and attitude that threatens to destroy my peace and steal my joy. Help me to never forget all of the blessings that you have given me. Open my eyes that I may focus more on your goodness and grace than anything else. AMEN.

WHO IS IN CHARGE?

"Meet every adverse circumstance as its master. Don't let it master you." - Anonymous

You still have choices. You still can respond to this terminality in a very positive and powerful way, or you can respond in a very negative and self-defeating way. The choice is up to you. The question you must ask yourself is, "who is in charge? Is it the disease, medication, doctor, family, nurse, friend, or death? It is true each of these do have some influence on your emotional, spiritual wellbeing, but they cannot dictate the direction of the soul. Even God does not force us to respond a certain way. He does not coerce his will on us. You must decide how you will respond to this difficult situation. It is up to you. Will you be its master or its slave?

Will you be the victim or the victor? Are you in charge or are your circumstances? You have a choice to choose how you will respond to life's circumstances. You can choose to be at peace with your challenges and difficulties. You can take charge of your feelings, beliefs, perspectives and dreams. No one or nothing can take these choices from you. You are in charge and you can make a difference in your life.

REFLECTIVE QUESTIONS

1. What do you still have control over?
2. What are some of the ways that you can change your life?

PRAYER

Oh God I thank and praise you for you are all powerful and almighty. So great is your power that you allow me to have power over my own life. Thank you for the choices, options the decision that you allow me to make. Grant me wisdom to make choice in accordance with your will. AMEN.

SITTING IN THE DARKNESS

"Though my soul may sit in darkness, it will rise in perfect light; I have loved the stars too fondly to be fearful of the night." – attributed to an aged astronomer

He sat at his wife's hospital beside for hours. It was 3 A.M., and he had not gone home in a couple of days. The lights were out, the television was off and darkness filled the room. I encouraged him to go home and get some rest, but, he refused, he said he wanted to be there in case his wife called out to him. Her husband wanted to stay with his wife. He did not want to go home. He seemed more distraught and discouraged than his dying wife. Suddenly she opened her eyes and told him," You need to go home now…I will be alright. I am not alone My God sits with me." Her husband was encouraged by her words and decided to go home. As we walked out the room he shared with me that he never thought about the fact that God was sitting with his wife. He said the thought that God was there comforting his wife was a comfort to him. He no longer had the depressing image in his head of his wife dying in a dark depressing room all by herself. He visualizes his wife sleeping peacefully as she holds the hand of our Lord. He said he could sleep now knowing that his wife was no longer sitting alone in darkness.

PRAYER

Almighty God you are the Light of the World. I am living in darkness. There is sadness, despair and the threat of death. Let your light shine down deep in my soul. Shine in my heart and soul. Let me experience your peaceful presence that I may let my light shine. Amen

REFLECTIVE QUESTIONS

1. Are you experiencing the darkness of despair?
2. What can you do to help someone who is living in darkness of despair?
3. Visualize God sitting at your bedside holding your hand. What do you think he would say to you?

HEAVEN NOW NOT LATER

"If what shows afar so grand, turn to nothing in thy hand, O again; the virtue lies in the struggle, not the prize". – R.M. Mines

Often, we anxiously anticipate the end of the death struggle and heaven's reward. We look forward to the moment when we will meet Jesus and he'll say to us, "Well done thou good and faithful servant…" We have read about a crown of righteousness, a mansion in glory and reward for the righteous. We wait for heaven.

However, we must realize that heaven is not just in the afterlife. It is right here and now. During your long suffering is heaven. For heaven is not just a place, it is perspective. Whenever we think of the goodness of God, we are in heaven. Whenever we can praise God for his presence during the struggle, we are in heaven. If we are in God and God is in us, we are in heaven. Therefore, we must have the faith to see the bliss in the burden and the serenity in the struggle. Gods favor is not just found in the future, but it is in the present. We need not wait for heaven. A piece of heaven is right here and right now. Every time we pray to God and commune with Him, we experience heaven.

REFLECTIVE QUESTIONS

1. What does it mean to be heavenly minded?
2. How can you experience heaven right here and now?

PRAYER

Oh Lord, I thank you for allowing me to experience heaven. Your loving presence and gracious spirit make me feel your glory. Your glory and victory is always with me and I will forever thank you. AMEN.

CIRCLE OF LOVE

"And let us not be weary in well-doing; for in due season we shall reap, if we faint not." – Galatians 6:9

Love is an eternal circle that never ends or begins. Whenever we give, it ultimately returns to us. The love, tears, care, nurturing, and sharing is not lost. It comes back to us in many ways and through many different people. Just because those who receive your love are either unable to respond or unwilling to reciprocate does not mean that it is not appreciated or will not be reciprocated. The long lonely hours spent at their death bed is seen by God and he has a way of replenishing and renewing your love. God will fill you with his love and grant you the strength to continue to love. Whatever you give will come back to you.

REFLECTIVE QUESTIONS

1. Do you feel that the love that you give is appreciate?
2. Do you feel that the love that you give is reciprocated?
3. Where do you see Gods love for you and your loved ones?
4. How is God replenishing your love?

PRAYER

God of love I am thankful for all the love that you bestow upon me. Your love sustains me, comforts me and empowers me to keep on loving. Help me to receive your love. Open my eyes that I see your love and open my ears that I can hear your love. Open my heart that I may receive your love and give it away. AMEN.

THE STING THAT SPRINGS

"Welcome each rebuff that turns earth's smoothness rough, each sting that bids not set not stand, but go." – Robert Browning

Death has a way of waking us up and activating our lethargic souls. It challenges us to make the best use of our time. We procrastinate plans, projects and promises. We defer dreams for a more "opportune time".

Ultimately, the death and dying experience stings our soul, pricks our conscience and ruffles our feathers so that we spring into action. Every sting, every bitter disappointment, painful feelings, physical malady should propel us to get fully involved with life. The sting of death is not meant to paralyze us in fear and apathy, it is meant to stimulate our faith into activity. The threat of death has a way of making us appreciate life and live it to the fullest. Therefore, we will rise from our apathy and complacency and do all that we can do.

REFLECTIVE QUESTIONS

1. What new ideas, thoughts or understandings have you learned?
2. How can this experience stimulate your faith?
3. What are some things that you need to do or say?

PRAYER

O Lord I thank you for waking up my sleeping soul so that I am more aware of your presence, your gifts and your blessings. Help me dear Lord to say and do all I need to do before this life ends. AMEN.

NO CROSS, NO CROWN

"There is always the battle to be fought before the victory is won. Too many think they must have the victory before the battle." – Dean Stanley

If there is no cross there will be no crown. It is one of life's inescapable truth. No matter who we are and what we have been able to accomplish, we will experience life's disappointments, trials and tribulations. There is no getting around the fact that we must go through the valley of the shadow of death before we get to green pastures and still waters. Good Friday's crucifixion will always precede Easter's resurrection. There is a battle to be fought and cross to bear before we receive God's crown.

It is the avoidance of the cross, of pain, struggle and death that produces the inner battle. The victory comes when we surrender ourselves to God. There will be no inner peace unless we are willing to fight the good fight. There will be no heavenly victory unless we are willing to defeat the devil. There is a price to pay for the crown that you will wear one day. You must be willing to deny yourself, take up your cross daily and present your body a living sacrifice. Once you do that, then the victory is ours!

REFLECTIVE QUESTIONS

1. Do you feel like you are victorious or defeated and why?
2. Have you surrendered yourself to God?
3. Are you willing to pay the price for your redemption?

PRAYER

Almighty God I surrendered my heart, my mind, my soul to you. I submit to my life to you. I trust you. Despite all of what I am going through I knew that God will give me the victory. Help me to bear my cross and fight the good fight. Give me the strength sacrifice and serve you with all that have. Empower me to pay the price as you have already paid the price for my redemption and victory. Amen

LAST STEP

"It is the last step in a race that counts; it is the last stroke on the nail that counts; many a prize has been lost just when it was ready to be plucked." - Anonymous

This episode in your life may be your last step. It may be your last day, the last time you may see your loved one or the last opportunity to commune with God. You must make your last step count because it will be the one that people will most remember. Your legacy that you leave with your loved ones is your last step. Tell someone that you love them, ask someone to forgive you, share your inner most thoughts with others, with God. Remember, it may be your last step. The last thing that you want to do is to take your life for granted. You cannot afford to waste any time with frivolous concerns and needs. You must prioritize the things in your life and do what is most important. These last days can be the most important days of your life. The right choices and actions determine your destiny. If you do what is pleasing in the eyes of God, it will mean you have crossed the finish line and receive a heavenly crown. However, if you squander your time and resources it will mean that you have fallen in the race and will receive eternal damnation. It would be tragic to have run the race of faith all your life and not finish. The race is almost over. It is not time to quit or be unfaithful now. Keep running until you cross the finish line in glory.

REFLECTIVE QUESTIONS

1. If you died tomorrow how would you like to be remembered?
2. What unfinished business do you have to do?
3. What could you do to please God?

PRAYER

Oh God I thank you for blessing me with my last step. Help me to make this day count. Help me to do what I need to do so help me not to waste a minute of the time that you give me. Please give me the wisdom to spend my time wisely and give you glory. AMEN

INTERESTING THOUGHTS

"The happiest people in the world are those who have the most interesting thoughts."- William Lyon Phelps

Our thoughts determine our happiness and peace of mind. Joy is not determined by external circumstances but an internal disposition. Your body can be deteriorating and dying, but your soul can be growing and glowing. A drab and dreary hospital room or nursing home cannot keep out joy. Joy finds the door of your mind, infiltrates it and provides interesting thoughts.

One of the most interesting thoughts is that you are God's child and God has not abandoned or forgotten you. God is standing right beside you telling you that everything is going to be all right. Another interesting thought is that you can experience paradise during your pain. Your paradise is the fact that God is with you. He is always present. He gives you strength during your weakness and joy despite your sorrows. One lost interesting thought is that there is a life beyond this life. There is external life with Jesus Christ. This is not the end of your life it is the beginning. Think about it. One day you will be at home with God, crowned with joy and wearing a robe of righteousness. One day there will be no diseases, no sickness, no suffering, no hospitals, doctors, or medicines. One day all you will experience is peace, joy, love, and righteousness. Think about it and make yourself happy.

REFLECTIVE QUESTIONS

1. Share some interesting thought that make you happy.
2. What do you think heaven is going to be like?

PRAYER

Oh God it is good to think about you and pray to you. Every time I think about your love and grace I smile. You love gives me joy that I need. Your love gives me joy that I need. Your grace leads me to glory. It leads me to my heavenly home. There is so much to think about. Thank you, Lord. Amen

THINK ON THESE THINGS

"Whatsoever things are true, whatsoever things are just, whatsoever things are pure, and whatsoever things are lovely, think on these things?" *(Philippians 4:8, 9)*

What are you thinking about? The doctor's diagnosis? The deadly disease ravishing your body? Are you filled with worry, doubt, fear, and despair? Are you thinking about the welfare of your loved ones? Are you thinking about death and dying? It is understandable and rational to think on those things that impact on your life. The question is, are you thinking about all of those things? Are you thinking about the positive as well as the negative? Are you always focused on your sorrows and not your joys?

You have the power to choose to think positive, joyful, and peaceful thoughts. You can discipline your mind to think on those things which are true, pure, and lovely. Think about the fact that God is true. His son Jesus Christ is the way, the truth and the life. He is the essence of that which is honest, truthful, and moral. Our God is just. God's sense of justice is best seen in the redemptive suffering of his son Jesus Christ. Jesus Christ was just, and he died for the unjust. Think about it. Our god is pure. There is nothing about him that is evil, wicked, or sinful. It is only through his holiness is not based on your religiosity but a relationship with Christ finally our God is lovely. Moreover, God is love. Think about the fact that God so loved you that he sacrificed Jesus Christ on the cross for our salvation. There is no greater thought than knowing that God loves you.

REFLECTIVE QUESTIONS

1. How foes the truth of God help you?
2. How does the purity of God help you?
3. How does the Love of God help you?
4. How does the justice of God help you?

PRAYER

Oh God I praise you. You and you alone are pure, just, lovely, and true. Help me to think about you. Help me to meditate on you. Give me positive prayers and uplifting thoughts. Amen

INDESTRUCTABLE

"No weapon that is formed against thee shall prosper, and every tongue that shall rise against thee in judgment thou shalt condemn. This is the heritage of the servants of the Lord, and their righteousness is from me," saith the Lord." (Isaiah 54:17)

Did you know that your soul is indestructible? There is nothing or no one that can destroy your soul. It is unbreakable, invincible and unconquerable. Its power, its strength, its ability to withstand life's destructible forces is found in God. God protects, shields and fortifies the soul against all satanic forces that threatens to undo it.

Often, we forget this truth. Our self-perception diminishes as we watch disease deteriorate our bodies. It is hard to believe you are indestructible when your body breaks down and you are unable to walk, talk and do things you used to take for granted. Sickness and suffering tend to make us feel hopeless, helpless, weak, and vulnerable.

Through it all, you must never forget that even though the body perishes, the soul lives on. Your soul can survive every weapon that the enemy uses. Thoughtless words, insensitive persons, poor medical care and devilish diseases cannot touch your soul. God has created your soul with an indestructible spirit. Your victory over everyone and everything is assured because God has made it so. So, keep your head up and know that your soul is undefeatable.

REFLECTIVE QUESTIONS

1. What are the forces that are attempting to destroy your body?
2. Do you realize that the body maybe destroyed but not the soul?
3. Do you realize that your soul is indestructible?

PRAYER

Oh God you are in destructible and unconquerable. Peace is no one or nothing greater than you. Help me to realize that if I live in you and you in me, I am indestructible. Lift my spirit that all who see me will know my spirit transcend the ravages of disease, despair, and death. Amen

INCOMPREHENSIBLE PEACE

"Be careful for nothing, but in everything by prayer and supplication, with thanksgiving, let your requests be made known to God; and the peace of God, which passeth all understanding, shall keep your hearts and minds through Christ Jesus." (Philippians 4:6, 7)

Are you worried? Are you feeling anxious and upset? Does the thought of death disturb your peace and trouble your soul? Do you feel as if you are on an emotional roller coaster and there is no stability to your life? One day you feel fine and the next day you feel miserable? Are you looking for peace that cannot be shaken or destroyed? The only one who can give you peace is almighty God. He is the prince of peace and he bestows an incomprehensible inner peace that no sickness, suffering or hardship can destroy. It is a peace that surpasses all understanding. It baffles doctors, mystifies clergy, and puzzles families and friends. They cannot understand how you can have this peace when you are going through so much.

Those who believe in the power of prayer, understand that God grants us this peace. As someone once said, "prayer does not always change things, but it changes us to meet the situation." Every time you talk to God and pour out your heart to him. Prayer is therapy for your mind and cleanses the soul of all its spiritual impurities such a bitterness, anger, and despair. Every time you thank God for all his blessings, it rekindles joy in your heart.

Prayer will give you a victorious grin during unbelievable odds. Only God can give you peace as you walk through the valley of the shadow of death. Only God can shield your heart from despair and sadness. Only God can protect your mind from negative thoughts and attitudes. He gives you a peace that the world did not give and cannot take away.

REFLECTIVE QUESTIONS

1. Do you have peace of mind? Why or why not?
2. What are the things that are robbing you of peace?
3. Have you discussed these things with God?

PRAYER

O God who is the Prince of Peace. Please give me thy peace that surpasses all understanding. Help me to put all my faith and trust in you so that all my fears, frustrations, and worries may decrease, and your presence and peace may increase. AMEN.

AUTUMN LEAVES

"Let life be beautiful like summer flowers and death like autumn leaves."- Tagore

You are an autumn leaf. You are colorful, beautiful and purposeful. The leaves must live for a period, but they also must fall. It is in their falling that their greater purpose is rendered. It is their task to reveal the tree, the source of their life. As an autumn leaf, you are called to reveal the tree or the wooden cross of Calvary. It is up to you to change, to get weak, fall and expose the source of your strength- Jesus Christ.

The death and dying process has a way of changing us. No matter how much we try to cover up, conceal and deny death, it inevitably changes us. There is nothing wrong with these changes. In fact it is natural for human beings to get old, weak, ill and die. We must begin to see ourselves like the autumn leaf. Our physical and emotional changes are a good thing. We should accept them and allow nature to take its place. As you see yourself changing and becoming weaker and weaker, know that you are becoming more and more beautiful. Realizing one day your beauty will manifest itself as you fall and expose the *Tree of Life*.

REFLECTIVE QUESTIONS

1. In what ways have you physically changed and how do you feel about it?
2. In what ways have you changed emotionally and how do you feel about it?
3. How has the death and dying process enable you to reveal Jesus Christ in your life?
4. What are the positive aspects of your changes?

PRAYER

Oh God of life who gives us life. We see your life in every season of life. In good and in bad times, in times of health and sickness, in times of strength and weakness you are forever with us. Help me to see and appreciate you during all of life's changes. Help me to testify of your goodness and grace through every transition. As I die and fall enable me to reveal the Tree of Life. Amen

FLY A KITE

"Adversity is the prosperity of the great. Kites rise against, not with, the wind." - Anonymous

It is time to fly a kite. It is time to allow your soul to soar higher on the winds of adversity. It is time to transcend your tragedy and let the world see the goodness of the Lord.

You are God's Kite and he desires for you to be a witness, a living testimony to His grace and courage. Through this sickness and suffering, others may be encouraged and strengthened. As you rise above your circumstances and give God praise, he is glorified. He is glorified in your gracious attitude and positive demeanor. Every time you publicly thank and praise God, you rise higher and higher. Let God fly his kite and one day, he will let go of the string.

REFLECTIVE QUESTIONS

1. How can this difficult experience empower you to get closer to God?
2. How can you allow God to be glorified in this experience?

PRAYER

Oh God I am your kite. I am your instrument of praise and glory. Please help me to transcend this tragedy that I may magnify you. I pray that when people look at me they see you in me. Let the words of my mouth and my demeanor, attitude and actions praise your holy name. AMEN.

WASTE NO TEARS

"Waste no tears over the grief's of yesterday." - Euripides

We can waste our time crying and grieving over yesterday's losses. Opening old wounds, retelling sad stories about past pain can be healthy to a certain degree, but it can be unhealthy when our tears blind us to today's blessings and bright future. One can be so focused in on their losses and not realizing the spiritual growth and gains that have come as a result of those losses. We can lose sight of God's grace that is present with us. Waste no tears over yesterday's losses when you have today's gains. You have something to be thankful about. Focus on God's blessings rather than life's burdens. Give God praise for every little thing that happens in your life.

REFLECTIVE QUESTIONS

1. Are you wasting tears?
2. Are you dwelling in self-pity?
3. What are some of the blessings that you still have?
4. What are you thankful for?

PRAYER

God of our weary years and God of our silent tears and any long days of grief and despair. Please wipe the tears from my eyes, lead my broken heart and comfort my wounded spirit. Give me your strength, your hope, and your joy. AMEN.

TEARS THAT HEAL

"Blessed are they that mourn; for they shall be comforted." (Matthew 5:4)

There are some people who mistakenly think that if they hold back their tears they will be healed. Others have bought into the false notion that if you are strong you will not cry. They think that tears are a sign of weakness, but nothing could be further from the truth. Tears are a sign that the healing process has begun in your life. The more you grieve the healthier you become. The more you mourn the more you are comforted. God will comfort you and heal your broken heart. As you shed your tears you will experience his care and compassion. He will heal your broken heart and wipe the tears from your eyes. God will let you know that you are not alone. He will never leave you or forsake you.

REFLECTIVE QUESTIONS

1. Do you think that if you cry you are weak?
2. Have you allowed yourself time and space to grieve?
3. Do you realize that God can comfort you as you grieve?

PRAYER

God of comfort and compassion I need your healing touch. My heart breaks, my soul aches and my tears are my companions. Please help me to cry. Give me the courage to let go of my tears that I may be healed. Please wipe away my tears an allow me to feel the joy of my salvation. Amen

NO FEAR

"People living deeply have no fear of death." - Anaus Nin

There is no reason to fear death. You have lived your life to the fullest. You have had a wealth of experiences. You have been on the mountain tops of joy and have been in the valley of sorrow.

There have been times in your life where you have been loved and admired. You have also, felt the sting of rejection and abandonment. You have shed tears of joy and your eyes have been red with anger. Life has had its ups and downs, therefore, there is no reason to fear death. It cannot take away any of your experiences. It cannot remove any of your rich memories. You have lived a full life and no one and nothing can take that from you. So, take time to reminisce about the good old days. Talk about the good and the bad times of your life. Reflect on the time when you first fell in love and all the relationships in your life. Recall the days of your youth and your high school experiences. Remember the days of your life when you struggled, fought and overcame the odds? Brag about your past accomplishments and achievements. What are some of those things that you are proud of? You have a great story to tell. It is the story of your life and no one else but you can share it. Even if no one wants to hear it you should take time to review it. Review your life and watch it as if you were watching a movie. Sit back close your eyes and enjoy watching your life.

REFLECTIVE QUESTIONS

1. What are some of the best experiences of your life?
2. What are some of the things that have given you great joy?
3. What are some of things that you have learned from life?
4. What are some of your fondest memories that you want others to know about?

5. What are the ways in which fear robs you of living life to the fullest?

PRAYER

Almighty God, you are the author and finisher of my faith. It is by your grace that you have written the story of my life. Thank you for a rich, full life. I am grateful for every memory which fortifies my faith and gives me the courage to live my life to the fullest. AMEN

FORGIVE THEM

"Father forgive them, for they know not what they do." (Luke 23:34)

The whole world was against him and yet he cried "Forgive them." The Scribes and Pharisees had persecuted vilified and condemned him. Yet he forgave them. The roman soldiers had spat on him, scourged, mocked, beat and crucified him. Yet he forgave them. His disciples had denied and abandoned him. Yet he forgave them. Why would anyone forgive someone who lied, criticized, and physically abused them? It does not make sense. Why did he do it?

Our Lord forgave them because there is divine power in forgiveness. The Greek word for forgive is *shaw* and it means to let go. When we forgive, we are letting go of our painful past with all of its insults, indignities and injustices. When we forgive, we let go of every evil thing that was said and done to us. Forgiveness means letting go of all evil, bitterness, anger and sadness and accepting Gods peace, strength, comfort, grace, and joy. Forgiveness means setting yourself free from your painful past and being able to enjoy your ultimate destiny in Gods goodness and righteousness. Jesus set himself free. How about you?

REFLECTIVE QUESTIONS9

1. Who do you need to forgive?
2. What painful past memories do you need to let go of?
3. What painful feelings do you need to let go of?

PRAYER

God of grace, mercy, and love help me to forgive and let go of all of my anger and bitterness. Give me the grace to let go of those painful memories and thoughts. Fill my mind with love and grace and forgiveness. Help me to let go of the thoughts of vengefulness and vindictiveness. Allow me to know of the grace of God that wipes the slate clean of all sin and evil. Help me to forgive and have mercy on their souls. As you forgive them, please heal me and forgive me that I may feel your loving embrace. AMEN

ACCEPTING MEANS ASSURANCE

"My grace is sufficient for thee, for my strength is made perfect in weakness." Most gladly therefore will I rather glory in my infirmities, that the power of Christ may rest upon me." (II Corinthians 12:9)

Paul the apostle prayed for God to remove his "thorn in the flesh". Biblical scholars state his "thorn" could have been his temper tantrums, seizures, handicap or even his false pride. Paul's "thorns" buffeted his body and bruised his spirit. He yearned to be liberated from it, but God's answer was "my grace is sufficient for you, for my strength is made perfect in weakness."

God reminded Paul that once he learned to accept his "thorn" he would discover God's grace and assurance. God assured Paul that his grace would compensate for any deficiencies. God's grace gives us strength for weakness, mercy for our sinfulness and serenity for our sorrows. God will answer your prayer. He may not answer it in the way and in the time that you want but He will answer prayer. God may not give you the miracle that you want but He will give you what you need. Therefore, you must learn to accept the unacceptable and tolerate the intolerable. It is in your acceptance of His will that you will discover His peace and joy.

REFLECTIVE QUESTIONS

1. What is your "thorn" in the flesh or your major weakness?
2. Have you learned to accept it? Why or why not?
3. Have you learned to accept death?
4. How has God's grace compensated for your weaknesses?

PRAYER

Lord I thank you for my thorn. I accept all of my weakness's faults, failures knowing that you have granted me your grace. And it is because of your grace that I have peace and strength. Thank you, Lord. AMEN!

I CAN SEE

"The Lord openeth the eyes of the blind, the Lord raised them that are bowed down, and the Lord loved the righteous." (Psalm 146:8)

There is a tendency to let grief and sorrow blind us of the grace and beauty of God. We can be so consumed in our despair that we can no longer see God's blessing and experience His joy. Some of us only see sickness or the disease. We are anxiously hoping and praying for healing. We constantly measure if we are getting better. Then there are others who only see darkness. They have become negative and cynical. They do not have anything positive to say about life. Death and dying has a way of blinding us of the truth. And what is the truth? The truth is that God is omnipresent and cares for us. The truth is that God is still blessing us in spite of death, disease, sickness, and suffering. The truth is that God gives sight to the blind and enables us to see His presence and power. We can see that He cares for us and heals us. When we humble ourselves and admit that we cannot see without Him, He gives us sight. We can see all of life's blessings and enjoy them. We can see and experience the miracle of life and death. With God I can see and praise His Holy name.

REFLECTIVE QUESTIONS

1. In what ways are you blind?
2. What are some of the good things that are happening in your life?
3. Where do you see the presence of God in your life?
4. What are the things that you focus most of your attention on and how can you refocus on God?

PRAYER

Almighty God, I humble myself before you. I admit that I cannot always see you or understand your will in my life. I confess my blindness and my inability to appreciate all of life's blessings. I have let my sorrows blind me of your goodness. I ask that you would heal me of my blindness that I may see you. Heal me to see you in spite of my sickness and sadness. Please give me sight that I may behold the beauty and majesty of your presence and peace. AMEN

YOU WILL NOT FALL

"Though he stumble, he will not fall, for the Lord upholds him with His hand." (Psalm 37:4)

We all stumble. Life has a way of tripping us up and making us fall. We stumble in broken relationships, financial troubles, work-related issues, poor decisions and immoral actions. The most devastating stumble is when the threat of death is upon us. When we realize that we or our loved ones is about to die, we stumble because we are afraid. We are afraid of dying. We do not want to die. We do not want to suffer. We are fearful for ourselves and for our loved ones. We stumble because of our doubts. We are full of doubts and anxiety. We don't know what will happen next or who we can depend on. We question everything and everybody. But our stumbling does not mean that we will fall. Our God is always there to keep us from falling into a pit of despair. His hand holds us and keep us from falling. We stumble but our God has our back. He knows how to strengthen our spirits and keep us going. When we grasp the hand of God we no longer stumble. All of our fears, doubts and despair dissipate. His hand gives us the courage and the faith to go forward. We might not know where the road of life may turn or how rough it will be. There are no guarantees that we will not stumble again, but this one thing we can be guaranteed is- that the hand of God will keep us from falling.

REFLECTIVE QUESTIONS

1. In what ways are you stumbling?
2. What kind of fears do you have?
3. What kind of doubts do you have?
4. What does holding the hand of God mean to you?

PRAYER

Almighty God I am stumbling. I am stumbling on my fears. I am so afraid of what may happen. Please give me your hand that I may have the faith to keep believing and walking and trusting in your presence and protection. Lord keep me from falling. Hold me with your tender hand. Let me find comfort in the hollow of your hand. As long as you hold me I will not fall. Amen.

HOPE IN GOD

"Why art thou cast down my soul? And why art thou disquieted within me? Hope thou in God, for I shall yet praise Him who is the health of my countenance, and my God." (Psalm 42:11)

The Psalmist does not understand the source of his sadness. He is reflective and remorseful. He asks, why am I downcast, why am I disturbed? Sometimes sadness can come upon us like a slow-moving fog. We are engulfed in a sense of hopelessness and despair. We cannot see any hope for a better day. And what is most devastating is we do not always know where it comes from. Sometime we know the source of sadness. It's the sickness. It's the disease. It's impending death. Even if we know where our grief stems from, we don't understand why we are still mourning. We think we have overcome it but it still persists. It dampens our spirits and our souls cry out for hope. The psalmist realized this and so he speaks to himself and says, "Put your hope in God." He realizes that he can choose to remain sad or have hope. He chooses to have hope in God. He understands that our only defense against the storm of despair is anchor of hope. Hope in God enables us to see through the fog of misery. Hope in God gives us the strength to go on. It enables us to give Him praise and thanks for all He has done. Place all your hope in God and He will end your sadness. Choose to Hope in God.

REFLECTIVE QUESTIONS

1. What are you sad about?
2. What is the source of your despair?
3. Are you willing to place your hope in God?
4. If you place your hope in God, how will your attitude be different?
5. If you place your hope in God, how will your behavior be different?
6. What choices can you make that reflect hope in God?

PRAYER

God of Hope I need you. I need your presence, power, and peace. I feel so sad, so depressed. I am filled with grief and despair. I don't see any hope for today or tomorrow. Help me to turn my focus from my sadness to my Savior. Let me place all of my faith and hope in you. Grant me a steadfast hope that I may praise you. Amen

KEEP MY LAMP BURNING

"For thou wilt light my candle: my God will enlighten my darkness."
(Psalm 18:28)

It maybe dark in your life. The threat of death can make your life feel dark and dreary. You may feel as if the lamp of your spirit is flickering and ready to be snuffed out. Your faith is weak and it is becoming harder and harder to believe. Each and every day your faith diminishes and your doubts increase. The lamp that is within you is almost out. The only one who can rekindle the flame is the Light of the world. His light will keep your lights burning. When you pray to God and commune with Him your light gets brighter and brighter. Your faith is restored and your hopes are renewed. The light has a way of making you believe again. We believe in God and God's care for us. We believe that deaths darkness cannot diminish the light. Doubt and despair no longer consume us. The light of God shines in us and around us. His light gives us the courage to face death and know that a new life awaits us. His light transforms our sadness into joy, our complaints into praise and our darkness into light. The more you pray to God the brighter your light becomes. His Light strengthens your light. His glory is your glory. His life means your life.

REFLECTIVE QUESTIONS

1. Are you living in darkness of despair?
2. Is your faith weak or strong?
3. How often do you pray to God?
4. What do you have to do to keep your light burning?
5. Do you have a positive attitude?
6. How can you help to rekindle someone else flame?

PRAYER

O Lord, Light of the world, keep my light burning. Let it not flicker in the darkness of despair. Keep me from thinking negatively and speaking pessimistically. Restore the flame of my faith. Keep my light burning that I may shine for you and that you may receive the glory. Amen.

HE IS LISTENING

"Then shall ye call upon me and ye shall go and pray unto me and I will hearken unto you." (Jeremiah 29:12)

God is listening. Sometimes we wonder if God is listening. We wonder if God will answer our prayers according to the time and way we want. When our prayers seem to go unanswered, we begin to doubt if God has heard us. It is hard to believe that God is listening when we continue to suffer. We reason, if my God is listening to my prayer then why am I still dying? Why has He not heard me? What we do not understand is that the very act of prayer is healing. The more we pray to God and share everything that is on our hearts the stronger our faith becomes. Prayer is therapeutic because it can heal us of our broken spirit. God encourages us to talk to Him because He knows that sharing your feelings is healing. God listens to everything that we have to say. We can tell him our anger, frustration, despair, bitterness, doubts, and hopelessness. If we need to curse at Him and tell Him how angry we are- He is listening. If we want to confess our doubts and disappointments in Him- He is listening. If you want to question His will in your life- He is listening. Our God loves us so much that He will listen to whatever we have to say and still love us. God loves us so much that He looks beyond all of our faults and sees our needs. So do not stop praying to God because He is listening. If you speak- He will listen and you will be healed.

REFLECTIVE QUESTIONS

1. Do you think that God is listening to you?
2. How would you feel if God doesn't answer your prayer?
3. Does unanswered prayer change your faith in God?
4. Have you shared all of your feelings and thoughts to God?
5. Do you realize that God is healing you while you pray?

PRAYER

O, Lord I do no pray to you enough. I admit that sometimes I wonder if you are listening. I keep praying and looking for answers but I don't see them. Please give me the faith to know that you are listening. For I know that you care about me and love me. Grant me the wisdom to know that as I pray to you are healing me and strengthening me. Help me to be honest with you and share all that is on my heart. For I know that you will hear the spirit beyond the words that I speak. I know it is not what I say that counts it's who I am in relation to you. I am your child and you are my Father. I thank you Heavenly Father for loving me and listening to me. Amen.

SWEET SLEEP

"When thou liest down, thou shalt not be afraid; yea thou shalt lie down, and thy sleep shall be sweet." (Proverbs 3:24)

It is time to sleep. Your body needs rest. Your mind requires peace. Your soul is tired and weary of the journey. In times like these that our God provides us with His sweet sleep. Sleep is sweet when we realize that God loves us and watches over us. Sleep is sweet when we know that we have nothing to be afraid of. The threat of death cannot disturb our sleep because our God gives us peace. The bitterness of life cannot take away this sweetness. There is serenity with God that surpasses all understanding. It is a sense of peace and inner tranquility. It rids us of all our fears. It removes all of our worries. It soothes us and relieves us of all our worldly concerns. God will give you sweet sleep when you lie down, close your eyes and count your many, many blessings. Sweet sleep comes to us when we think about how good God has been. So, go ahead and go to sleep. It is God's gift to you. It is His way to bless you and heal you. Enjoy His sweet sleep. For one day you will sleep into glory and you will awaken in the arms of our God.

REFLECTIVE QUESTIONS

1. Is it too difficult to sleep?
2. What keeps you up at night?
3. When you go to sleep do you count your blessing?
4. When you go to sleep can you imagine being cradled in the arms of God?

PRAYER

O' Lord you have blessed me with sweet sleep. As I lay down to sleep, help me to think about you and all that you have done for me. Help me to count all of my blessings and go to sleep with praises on my lips. For you O' Lord gave me peace, comfort and joy. It is because of you that I can go to sleep knowing that you will watch over me. Thank you, Lord for all that you have done and are doing. I will sleep well because I know you have me in your arms. Amen

MY ROCK

"The Lord is my rock, and my fortress and my deliverer, my God my strength, in whom I trust. My buckler and the horn of my salvation, my Hightower." (Psalm 18:2)

The death and dying process has a way of draining all of the strength and faith out of you. The body deteriorates and gets increasingly weak. The spirit gets deflated and the soul becomes defenseless. Every day it becomes harder and harder to defend yourself from the demons of despair that bring you down. You get tired. Tired of keeping up appearances. Tired of fighting. Tired of believing. Tired of trying to be strong for everyone else. Tired of all the doctors, medicines, family, friends, clinicians that offer help but cannot help you in the fight for your soul. The only one who can and will fight for your soul is God. Only God has the strength to deliver you from the onslaught of demons. Only God can be your rock, fortress and refuge. Our God is all powerful and all mighty and there is no one else like Him. Only God can shelter you from the storms of life and fight the demons of despair. When you are weak your spirit must cling to Him. Pray to Him. Hold onto Him. He is your rock. He will be your strength. You can find faith and courage in Him. God will renew your spirit. He will transform your fatigue to faith, your weakness into strength and your tired spirit into a spirit of victory. The battle is not yours. It is the Lords'. He will fight your battle. When you are no longer able to fight. God will fight. When your back is against the wall, He will protect you. When you are tired of being tired. God will be your rock and your refuge. The victory is yours if you remember that the battle is the Lords. He is your Rock and Refuge.

REFLECTIVE QUESTIONS

1. In what ways are you tired?
2. What are you tired of?

3. What are you fighting?
4. Have you prayed to God for strength and courage?

PRAYER

O God, my rock, my refuge I am so tired. Tired of death and dying. Tired of worrying and waiting and wondering. I am tired of the fight and can no longer fight-on. I need you. I need your strength, your power, your presence to fight this battle. Grant me the wisdom to discover that only when I am weak then I am strong in you; and only when I can no longer fight, you will fight my battles; and only when I surrender can I find victory in you. Amen.

WHAT DO YOU SEE?

"Now faith is the substance of things hoped for, the evidence of things not seen." (Hebrews 11:1)

"For we walk by faith, not by sight." (II. Corinthians 5:7)

What do you see? Do you see death, disease, pain, suffering and loss? Or do you see life, heaven, happiness and loveliness? Do you see all of the negative aspects of life or do you see the positives? Can you see God at work in your life or is He absent or nonexistent? It is all a matter of faith or perspective. Faith is seeing the invisible, believing the unbelievable and tolerating the intolerable. Faith is seeing the hand of God at work in your life. It is knowing that God is providing for you and watching over you. Your faith is a critical factor in your life. It can determine how you will feel, what you will believe and how you will live. The measure of faith you have makes all the difference in the world. If you have a little faith, you will have a little result. If you have great faith, you will have great results. So, what you see in your life is really about your faith. If you want to change your life you must change your faith. You must choose to see heaven in the midst of hell, life in the midst of death, and have joy in spite of sorrow. It's really up to you. See whatever you choose to see.

PRAYER

O' Lord grant me faith to see you in my life and in the life of others. Let me see your hand at work in my life. Bless me with the vision to see victory over disease, death and loss. Allow me to see all of life's beauty and blessings. Grant me the eyes to see all of your goodness, mercies and love. Open my eyes that I may see you in life and in death.

REFLECTIVE QUESTIONS

1. What do you see in your life?
2. Name some positive things that are happening in your life?
3. Where do you see the hand of God at work in your life?
4. How has this death and dying experience blessed you?

FAITHFUL TO THE FAITHLESS

"If we believe not, yet he abided faithful, He cannot deny Himself." (II. Timothy 2:13)

It is hard to keep the faith when you are dying. Impending death has a way of blasting all of our hopes and shattering our dreams. We doubt God and His will in our lives. We question whether God cares for us while we suffer. We even get angry with God because of all the underserved and unjust suffering. It upsets us to see so called evil people prospering and just people dying. Life doesn't make sense. It doesn't go as we planned and we lose faith. We become cynical, faithless. We no longer trust God. We can't believe in Him anymore. But the good news is even thou we are faithless, God is faithful. Even thou we have our doubts about God, He continues to believe in us. In spite of all of our angry curses of God, He still loves us. God is faithful to us even when we are faithless to Him. He doesn't abandon us or reject us just because of our doubts. God doesn't turn His back on us just because we have stopped praying and believing. He can no more reject us than He can Himself. God is bound to us by His unbreakable unconquerable love. His love will not let us go. God will always love us no matter what we say or do. It is in His nature to love us unconditionally. We may not love Him or have our doubts about Him, but one thing we can be sure of, He always loves us and believe in us.

REFLECTIVE QUESTIONS

1. In what ways are you faithless?
2. Do you have doubts about God and His will in your life?
3. In what ways do you see God taking care of you?
4. How is God faithful to you?
5. How can you be more faithful to God?
6. How is God loving to you?

PRAYER

God of love who is faithful to all of your children. I confess my faithlessness, my doubts and my negative spirit. Forgive me for not believing in you, even when you believed in me. Have mercy on my soul for not having faith and trust in you. Grant me a faith that will believe no matter what happens to me in life. Enable me to be faithful as you are faithful. Empower me with a love that will not let me go. Amen.

UNSHAKEABLE LOVE

"For the mountain shall depart and the hills be removed, but my kindness shalt not depart from thee, neither shall the covenant of my peace be removed," saith the Lord, that hath mercy on thee." (Isaiah 54:10)

There is nothing more earthshaking then the unanticipated death of a loved one. It shakes the very foundation of our faith in God. It can make us question God, our loved ones, health care persons and even ourselves. It is hard to accept this kind of change, especially when it comes unexpectedly. This kind of abrupt change robs us of our peace of mind and makes life feel so unstable. The only one we can rely on is almighty God. The love of God is unshakeable, indestructible and indivisible. There is nothing or no one that can shake the love of God. Disease cannot deteriorate it, sickness cannot shake it. Suffering cannot break it, death cannot destroy it. God's love is unshakeable. You might not be able to count on family, friends, healthcare professionals, or your plans for the future, but you can count on the love of God. His compassion and commitment will remain with you till the end of time. He will never leave or let you go because His love is unshakeable.

REFLECTIVE QUESTIONS

1. What changes have you had to endure?
2. How have you been shaken?
3. How has God's love given you a sense of security?
4. How has God's love given you a sense of stability?

PRAYER

God of love, hear the prayer of your child who has been shaken by the changing circumstances of life. I have been shaken by sickness, loss and the thoughts of death. But I trust in your unfailing, unshakeable love. Your love keeps me strong and steady. Your love gives me a sense of security and stability. Amen.

GOD LOVES YOU

"For God so loved the world that he gave his one and only begotten son that who so ever believeth in Him should not perish but have everlasting life." (John 3:16)

There are those who may ask, "Does God love me?" They have serious doubts about the love of God because they see so much pain and suffering. It may be hard to believe in the love of God when you or your loved one is slowly dying. It may be difficult to believe in God's compassion when your prayers seemed to go unanswered. Where is the love of God when death is imminent? Where is the mercy of God when the pain is unbearable? If you want to know where the love of God is, look no further than the cross on which Jesus was crucified. The ultimate expression of God's love for us is the sacrificial redemptive death of Jesus. God's love for us is so great that He would sacrifice His only son so that we may have everlasting life. If you want to know if God loves you look at and believe in Jesus. God has already demonstrated His love. His love allowed His son to die a painful, inhumane death. Jesus knows the excruciating pain and loss that you feel. He knows what you are going thru, believe in Him, believe in Him that you may know God's love for you. Believe in the redemptive death of Jesus that you may have life everlasting. Believe in Jesus and believe that God loves you.

REFLECTIVE QUESTIONS

1. Why do you believe in God's love?
2. What makes you doubt God's love?
3. How does God demonstrate His love for you?
4. Do you believe in Jesus Christ died for your sins and was resurrected from the grave?

PRAYER

God of love heal my broken heart with your love. Let your love heal me of all my doubts, fears, anger and worries. Give me faith that I may believe in your son Jesus Christ. Allow me to experience your love through Him and with Him. Grant me eternal life through Jesus Christ. Amen.

BURDEN BEARER

"Come to me, all you who are weary and burdened and I will give you rest." (Matthew 11:28)

Carrying the burden called death can drain you spiritually and emotionally. Thinking about death and dying is exhausting. It makes your faith weak and it can make you unable to cope with life. It breaks your heart with sadness and sorrow. It weighs you down and you feel like giving up and surrendering to the inevitable. At times like this we need to admit that we are not strong enough to carry this heavy burden. We need to give this burden to the Burden Bearer who will gladly bear it for us. Whenever we pray to God and share all of our worries, fears, doubts, guilt, anger, and sorrows He will heal us. He frees us of the burden so that we may find peace and rest in Him. Giving your burden to God is a great relief. You will discover an inner tranquility and serenity that only He can give. He is a Burden Bearer and He invites you to give Him your burdens. If you need rest give God your burdens. Share all your thoughts and feelings to God.

REFLECTIVE QUESTIONS

1. Why is death a burden to you?
2. What makes the threat of death so draining?
3. Have you prayed to God and told him how you feel?
4. If you gave your burden to God how would you feel?
5. Have you experienced the rest that is found in God?

PRAYER

O' Lord I'm tired of carrying this heavy burden. It is just too much to bear. Take this burden called death that I may rediscover life in you. Free me of this burden that I may have peace and comfort in you. Amen.

TRUST IN THE LORD

"Trust in the Lord with all thine heart and lean not unto thine own understanding; in all your ways acknowledge him, and He will direct thy paths." (Proverbs 3:5, 6)

It is hard to trust God when you do not know why you are suffering and dying. It is hard to understand and accept His will. Sometimes it does not make sense. We question God and ask Him why and we never seem to receive a good answer. Life can be so unfair sometimes. Life's unfairness can fill us with doubts, despair and frustration.

We must learn to trust in the Lord. We must have faith in the goodness of God and His unconditional love. We can trust God because whatever He does stems from love. It is in His nature to love and therefore God is always loving. We might not feel His love but that does not deny the fact that He loves us. We can trust in the Lord because He is omniscient all wise. God knows our daily struggles, trails, and tribulation. God knows exactly what we are going through and He knows what is best for us. All of our difficulties will ultimately be used for our spiritual good and growth. We can only see a small picture of life's puzzle. Our perspective is limited. But God see's the entire picture. His perspective is broad and all encompassing. From God's perspective, your entire life is a beautiful masterpiece. What you may see as a mess on the canvas of your life is all a part of the bright beautiful portrait of your soul. What you may see as a detour on the road of life will lead in the paths of righteousness. So, trust in the Lord and you will be blessed.

REFLECTIVE QUESTIONS

1. Do you have a difficult time with the will of God?
2. Why is it hard for you to trust in the Lord?
3. Name some good reasons to trust God.

PRAYER

O' Lord help me to trust in you. I acknowledge that I do not understand why this happening to me. But I trust that you know what is best for me. Grant me more faith as I follow you and seek your will in my life. Amen.

NO MORE CRYING

"And God shall wipe away all tears from their eyes. There shall be no more death neither sorrow nor crying neither shall there be any more pain, for the former things are passed away." (Revelations 21:4)

It is alright for you to cry. It is perfectly natural for you to grieve for yourself and others. We all shed tears in our own way and in our own time. It is perfectly human for you to get sad, depressed and even wallow in self-pity. No one can tell you not to cry or feel sorry for yourself. They do not know what you are feeling and what you are really going through. You not only have the right to your tears you have the responsibility to yourself to shed them. So, if you want to have a pity party go ahead and have one. It's your life, your heart and your tears.

However, there will come a time when you will no longer shed tears. There will be a day when God will wipe away all of your tears and there will be no sickness, disease or death. God understands all of the pain and suffering that you are feeling. He knows your daily struggle and brokenness. He hears your prays and cry for help. God is with you. He will cry when you cry. He will mourn when you mourn and in the process of your grieving God will comfort and strengthen you. He will give you the grace to cry and grace to go on. God will ensure that in glory you will no longer cry. He promises you that you will no longer cry, mourn, or feel sad. He will give you peace, joy and love. For in heaven there will be no more crying, no more tears, only laughter and smiles in heaven.

REFLECTIVE QUESTIONS

1. What are you sad about?
2. Do you take time to cry? Why or why not?
3. What are you feeling?

4. How has God comforted you and how can you comfort someone else?

PRAYER

God of our weary years and God of our silent tears, please hear my cry. I long for peace, comfort, and rest. My soul grows weary of this long struggle. Heal me of my brokenness and weakness. Wipe the tears from my eyes and mend my broken heart. Amen.

THE GIFT OF GOD

"For the wages of sin is death, but the gift of God is eternal life through Jesus Christ our Lord." (Romans 6:23)

Have you discovered or opened your gift? God has a gift for you. It is wrapped in a fleshly package called Jesus Christ. Jesus Christ is the gift of God. A gift is not something that you earned, achieved or purchased. A gift is something that is given to you with no price tag attached. God has given you His Son Jesus Christ and Jesus paid the price by suffering and dying on the cross for our redemption. Jesus is a gift because we did not deserve Him or achieve Him. God gave us the gift of His Son because He loved us. The great thing about this gift is the eternal life that we receive through Him. In other words when we die in this life God will give us eternal life. We will go to glory and find eternal bliss in Heaven. All we have to do to open this gift is repent of our sins and accept Jesus Christ as our Lord and Savior. To unwrap this precious package, you must unwrap your heart. You must open yourself to the spirit of God and let God begin to change you from the inside out. If you receive and open this gift of God called Jesus Christ you will receive forgiveness of your sins, redemption for your soul, peace of mind that surpasses all understanding, eternal life, a house with many mansions, a crown of life and a robe of righteousness. But the most wonderful aspect of God's gift is Jesus Christ Himself. Once you meet Him you will never be the same.

REFLECTIVE QUESTIONS

1. Have you opened God's gift to you?
2. Have you taken time to repent of your sins and accept Jesus Christ as your Lord and Savior?
3. Do you want to go to Heaven?
4. Have you opened your heart to God to receive His Son Jesus Christ?

PRAYER

Almighty God, I thank and praise you for the gift of your only begotten son Jesus Christ. I want to receive this gift. Please forgive me for all of my sins and short comings. I accept Jesus as my Lord and savior. I ask Him to come into my heart that I may know Him, love Him and be with Him in heaven. Amen.

PERFECT PEACE

"Thou will keep him in perfect peace whose mind is stayed on thee, who trust thee." (Is.26:3)

If there is one thing that we all have in common, one thing that we all desire and that is peace of mind. We all want a sense of peace and contentment. We all desire a sense of inner tranquility and emotional stability. We want peace at home, at work, in our community, in our world and especially in our hearts. Yet if there is one thing that many people lack is peace. Paschal stated that, "The reason we don't have peace in the world is because a man cannot sit in a room all alone." We lack peace and are under enormous amounts of stress and pressure. The terminally ill are especially struggling with a lack of inner peace. The threat of death robs them of peace and steals their joy. Some of them struggle with pain, physical limitations, loneliness, anger, guilt and hopelessness.

As a hospice chaplain I saw this elderly woman in her nursing home room crying out in enormous pain. She begged me to get a nurse to receive her pain medication. I immediately told a nurse who indicated that she was busy with other patients and would come see her as soon as she could. I went back to the room and told the woman that the nurse was on the way. The woman had tears in her eyes as she shared how much pain she was in. I held her hand and began to recite the 23rd Psalm. The woman closed her eyes and began to recite it with me. She began to calm down. She no longer cried out in pain. She stopped crying. By the time I finished reciting the psalm she was at peace. The nurse finally came in to give her the pain medication but God had already gotten there before the nurse to give her peace. This woman found peace when she began to focus on God.

REFLECTIVE QUESTIONS

1. What robs you of peace of mind?
2. Have you tried to focus your attention on God rather than your worries or concerns?
3. Have you tried to count your blessings rather than think about your burdens?

PRAYER

God grant me the peace that only you can give and the world cannot take away. Amen

FORSAKEN BUT NOT FORGOTTEN

"My God, My God, Why, hast thou forsaken me?" (Matthew 27:46)

It may be hard to believe but Jesus Christ the Son of the living God felt forsaken, abandon by God. How could this be? How is it that the co-creator of the heavens and the universe could be rejected by the Creator? Was it not the Heavenly Father who said to Jesus at his baptism, "This is my son in whom I am well pleased?" Did not the Heavenly Father anoint His son to heal the sick, exorcise demons, feed the multitudes, walk on water and raise the dead? If Jesus did all of these miracles to glorify his Heavenly Father, why is His Heavenly Father abandoning him now? It does not make sense.

Nor does it make sense when we feel forsaken and abandoned by God. We think that just because we feel lonely that God has forsaken us. We reason that if we are still in pain God has not answered our prayers. Like our Lord we naturally feel alienated from God and this maybe the greatest challenge to our faith. For there is nothing more devastating than feeling that God is not there for you. But the fact that Jesus shares his despair from the cross reveals that God understands when we feel lonely and forsaken. God knows what you are going through. He will dry the bitter tears from your eyes. He will comfort you in your affliction. He will strengthen you in your weakness. Moreover, the fact that Jesus cries out to God reveals the reality of our God. God is real even when we don't see him or feel Him. We may not see Him but He sees us. We may not hear Him but He hears us. We can express our loneliness and despair knowing that God will answer our prayer in His own time and in His own way. We may feel forsaken but we are not forgotten. God heard Jesus prayer and He will hear yours.

REFLECTIVE QUESTIONS

1. Do you feel lonely?
2. Do you feel forsaken by God?
3. In what ways do you see God at work in your life?
4. Have you expressed your true feelings to God?

PRAYER

Almighty God, where are you when I need you the most? Please give me the eyes to see you and the ears to hear you and the heart to feel your loving presence. Amen

LEARNING TO DIE

"While I thought that I was learning how to live. I have been learning how to die." Leonardo Da Vinci

Do you know how to die? This is quite a provocative and challenging question. We spend our entire lives learning how to live and avoiding dying. Many people try desperately to live healthy, productive and prosperous lives. The last thing many of us want to do is to endanger ourselves, contract an illness and die a premature death. We spend a lot of our time educating ourselves, gathering wisdom, amassing knowledge on how to live and we must be just as intentional and purposeful in learning how to die. Every day we must take the opportunity to learn from death. Death instructs us on what is important and what is trivial. Death helps us to set priorities in our lives. We are no longer consumed about superfluous, shallow, transitory issues and concerns. We know what we want and desire out of life. We learn how to die by letting go of superficial needs. All of the material possessions and property are not essential to us. The home, car, clothes, property and possessions no longer hold value for us. We learn when we let these things go. We learn how to die when we no longer take our loved ones for granted. The more you respect death the more you respect and cherish your life or your loved ones. You can let go of any bitterness and anger against them. We learn how to die when we understand that real life is beyond the grave. We no longer have to fight to stay alive. We understand that a life of love, peace and joy awaits us. The day we die is the day we cease from learning and graduate from death to eternal life.

REFLECTIVE QUESTIONS

1. What are your priorities?
2. What are the things that you need to let go of?

3. Who have you taken for granted and what will you do or say when you see them again?
4. What superficial needs, concerns, and possessions do you need to let go of?
5. What is death teaching you?

PRAYER

God of the Resurrection and the Life I am ignorant of death and eternal life. Educate me on death and grant me wisdom to appreciate every day that you bless me with. Teach me about the preciousness of life that I may not squander it. Help me not to take my life and the lives of others for granted. Prepare my mind and heart to graduate and live with you. Amen

READY TO GO

"Death never takes the wise man by surprise; He is always ready to go."
Jean Da La Fontaine

Are you ready to go? Are you ready to die? You may say, "No I am not ready to die. I don't want to leave my family and friends. I am afraid to die. "Or some may say, "I don't want to die. I am going to fight every moment of my life to stay alive. I refuse to give up. I refuse to lie down and die. I want to live."

It does not matter if we fight to live or if we are afraid to die. The fact of the matter is that we are going to die. There is nothing or no one that will stop death from coming. The question is not are you going to die, the question is are you ready to die?

The only way to get ready to die is to accept that you will die. The day will come when you will breathe your last breath and you will cease to exist. Death is life's common denominator. We will all die and it is just a matter of time. The only thing that you can do is get ready for it. Getting ready to die is like getting ready to make a long trip. When you take a trip you pack your bags and carry all your necessities. Likewise, you must pack your spiritual suitcase when you are taking a heavenly trip. What you need in your spiritual suitcase are the garments of gratitude. Every time you express your gratitude or see the positive side of things you are packing garments of gratitude. Your spiritual suitcase requires the clothes of compassion. Showing love to family and friends is a way of getting ready to die. Also, forgiving those who have hurt us in the past prepares us for the future.

Packing the clothes of compassion and the garments of gratitude in your spiritual suitcase prepares you for deaths journey. Every day you can find an opportunity to be thankful and to show love. Every day you have the opportunity to get ready to die. So, pack your bags and get ready to go.

REFLECTIVE QUESTIONS

1. Are you ready to die? Why or why not?
2. What is the unfinished business that you need to do before you die?
3. What are some of the things that you are thankful for?
4. How could you show more love?
5. Are there any broken relationships that you need to repair before you die?

PRAYER

God I'm not ready to die. I still want to live. Please help me to get ready to die. Grant me the grace to pack my bags and get ready to go to heaven. Help me to show more love and kindness to everyone I meet. Open my eyes that I can be thankful for all the blessings in this life. Amen

ANSWERS TO QUESTIONS

"Seek ye first the Kingdom of God and His righteousness and all these things shall be added unto you." (Matt. 6:33)

When we are in the fight for our lives our minds entertain a host of seemingly unanswerable questions. What did I do to deserve this? Why am I sick and suffering? Why do good people suffer and evil people prosper? Why is this happening now? What can I do to get out of this mess? When will God heal me? How can I cope with this? What will tomorrow bring?

These questions and many others torment our hearts and erode our peace. Unfortunately, there are no easy answers. Most of these questions will be answered in eternity. But some questions are answerable if we only turn to almighty God. God not only has the answers to our questions, He is the answer. It is in Him that we discover the will of God for our lives. When we look to God for the answers to our questions, we are given the assurance that His will be done. He comforts us and enables us to accept the unacceptable. He strengthens us in our weakness and despair. All of our questions may not be answered but His presence in our lives gives us peace.

REFECTIVE QUESTIONS

1. What are the debilitating questions that drain you?
2. What are you angry or disappointed about?
3. How does the presence of God give you peace even in the midst of your troubles?

PRAYER

O Lord I seek you to answer my questions. I have faith that you know what is best for me but I still have doubts. I still have questions. Help me to put all of my faith and trust in you. For you are an all wise, all knowing God who has my best interest at heart? So, I thank you for being the answer to my prayers. Amen

OUT OF HELL

"Death is for many of us the gate of hell; but we are inside on the way out, not outside on the way in." George B. Shaw

There is a heaven and there is a hell. For some people these realities are not places in eternity. They are not some ethereal place where our souls go for eternal bliss or condemnation. For some people heaven and hell can be experienced here on earth. There are those who are experiencing a living hell. Fire and brimstone is nothing compared to the daily pain and anguish they feel. Its hell to become physically disabled and watch your body fall apart and become completely dependent on others. It is hell to be unable to speak your mind and share how you really feel and what you need. To be completely incapacitated and unable to move is a living hell. It is like being a prisoner of your own body. There is no freedom, no joy and no peace, but there is an escape from this earthly hell. It is called death. Contrary to popular opinion death is not a terrible reality. Nor is it a gateway into nothingness. It is a doorway into heaven. Death is not the end of existence; it is the beginning of life. When we die we shall leave this wicked world of pain and suffering. We shall be set free from the ills of this existence. We will be out of hell and into heaven. Heaven will be a place of joy and laughter. There will be no pain, suffering or sickness in heaven. Our souls will finally be set free from our dying decaying bodies. We will be liberated from all burdens and cares of this world. We have much to look forward to. When we die we will leave hell and go to heaven.

REFLECTIVE QUESTIONS

1. Do you believe in heaven and hell? Why or why not?
2. How has life been a living hell for you?
3. What do you think will happen to you when you die?
4. How will death be a blessing for you?

PRAYER

Almighty and merciful God I can no longer cope with all of this pain and suffering. I am living in hell. I yearn to escape this tormented existence. Be merciful to me and let me die that I may be ushered into heaven. Amen

HAPPY BIRTHDAY

"The day which we fear as our last is but the birthday of eternity." Seneca

You have a birthday coming. It is not the day of your birth, it's the day of your death. On the day that you die you will be born again to a life beyond this life. The body will die but your soul will live again in eternity. Your soul will live forever in a place where there is no pain, suffering, sickness, disease or death. Your soul will smile and laugh again. You will know peace and harmony with the universe. Your death will be the ultimate birthday party of all time. For you will not only celebrate your new life but all of those deceased loved ones will celebrate with you.

Therefore, do not be discouraged by death and dying process. It may be painful but it will have a joyful ending. We should see the dying process like a woman in child birth. The labor pains are unbearable but the beauty of the newborn makes it all worth it. As you endure the pain of dying know that one day your body will give birth or release your soul. And your soul will not be crying, you will be smiling. You will be full of life and laughter. For it is your birthday. Happy birthday!!

REFLECTIVE QUESTIONS

1. What could you do to prepare your soul for its ultimate birthday celebration?
2. What do you think eternity will be like?
3. What deceased loved ones will be celebrating your birthday with you?

PRAYER

God of life I thank you for life. I praise you for every day and year that you have blessed me to live. Help me to understand and accept the fact that death is not the end of my life, it is the beginning. Give me the faith to believe that my death is not a time for mourning but celebration. It is a birthday party with all those who have died before me. Amen

WOUNDED HEALER

"But he was wounded for our transgressions, he was bruised for our inequities; the chastisement of our peace was upon him and with his stripes we are healed." (Isaiah 53:5)

Jesus Christ is the Wounded Healer. He was mocked, beaten, spat on, whipped, stabbed and crucified for our redemption. His physical wounds mean our spiritual healing. It is in Him and through Him that we receive forgiveness of our sins and shortcomings. It is because of Him that we are reconciled to all mighty God. Our Heavenly Father accepts us because Jesus Christ took the eternal punishment for our transgression. Our God forgives us of all of our sins, addictions, attitudes, vices, weaknesses, lust, pride, greed, violence, anger, and unfaithfulness. In forgiving us of our evils God heals us and we discover His peace. This peace surpasses all understanding. We may not understand it but through Christ we can be at peace with God, others and ourselves. We no longer have to be full of guilt and shame. Self-hatred and self-reproach will not be a part of our identity. Since God has forgiven us, we can forgive ourselves. We experience the unconditional love and acceptance of God. We can be at peace with others because Christ teaches us to love others regardless of who they are and what they have done. We no longer have to harbor anger, bitterness and vengefulness. We will have His love in us. Finally we can have peace with death because through Jesus Christ we have eternal life. We don't have to be afraid of dying because another life awaits us. We will be reunited with our loved ones and we will experience heaven in all of its beauty and holiness. Moreover, we will be face to face with the one who forgave us, healed us and redeemed us. We will see the wounded healer himself … Jesus Christ.

REFLECTIVE QUESTIONS

1. What are your inner spiritual wounds?

2. What is it that is troubling you?
3. Have you discovered forgiveness of sins through Jesus Christ?
4. Have you asked Jesus Christ to heal you of your inner wounds?

PRAYER

O Lord, I have so many inner wounds, brokenness, sin and sorrow. I need you to forgive me of my sins and be my Lord and Savior. Please heal my wounded spirit, bind my broken heart, and grant me your peace. Heal me lord by your grace and mercy. Let me experience your unconditional love that I may have peace with you, others and myself. Amen

GREATEST BLESSING

"Death maybe the greatest of all human blessings." Socrates

Is death a burden or blessing? Some perceive death as a horrendous burden that crushes the human spirit. But we should not see it that way. Death is not a burden. It can be seen as the greatest of all blessings. It enriches our soul in many ways. Death is a physician because it ends all of our bodily diseases. It is a therapist because when we die all tears and sadness are vanquished. Death is a liberator because it sets us free from this wicked world. We are no longer shackled by our weaknesses, vices, addictions and transgressions. Death blesses us with prosperity. Our souls become rich in eternity's blissfulness. We shall enjoy the inexpressible joy and peace of God's presence. Death blesses us with a new life where we will experience heaven in all of its glory and beauty. Death is truly the greatest of all human blessings. For it means our ultimate healing, salvation and liberation. But more than that it means that we will see our Savior face to face.

REFLECTIVE QUESTIONS

1. What kind of blessing do you think death will give you?
2. What are the benefits or blessing of dying?
3. How can you change the way you think about death?

PRAYER

God of bountiful blessings, you continue to bless me in so many ways. I did not realize that even death can be a blessing in my life. I thought that dying is the worst thing that could happen to me. Now I understand that when I day I will be blessed in so many ways. Thank you for all that you have done in my life and when I die. Amen

TODAY YOU LIVE

"No one can confidently say that we will still be living tomorrow." Euripides

Today you are alive. Tomorrow is not promised to you. The only thing that you can be guaranteed is the life that you have right now. It might not be the kind of quality of life that you want. You may have sickness and suffering but you still have life. You might not be able to walk and talk like you used to, but you still have life. You may feel weak, worthless and helpless but you still have life. As long as you have life you still have infinite value. As long as blood courses through your veins you are a precious child of God. Therefore, live your life to the fullest.

I knew of an eighty-three years old who lived her life to the fullest. She had stomach cancer, high blood pressure, and had several heart attacks. Her stomach was removed and she lost over forty pounds. She was weak and frail and struggled to do simple tasks. She had survived the untimely death of her son. Her house burned down to the ground and she lost all of her personal possessions. In spite of all of her losses she refused to give up on life. She still lived independently by herself. She still went shopping at the thrifty stores. She drove her car wherever and whenever she wanted to. She still had a great sense of humor and a feisty spirit. She was a community activist and campaigned for President Obamas reelection. She was active in her church as missionary and spiritual mother. I asked her, "What keeps you going? "She held her head up and boldly proclaimed that her motto was" either you better get busy dying or living, and I'm determined to live as long as I can!

This elderly sickly woman was an inspiration to her family, her church and her community. Her life was a living testimony of the grace of God at work. She showed the world not to take life for granted. Life is too short. We must live it to the fullest. We cannot afford to waste any time. Live your life as if each day maybe your last. For it is not how long you live but how well.

PRAYER

Oh God you are our Alpha and Omega, you are the beginning and the ending. Help me to live this life and enjoy every minute of it. Give me the grace to appreciate whatever I have and do whatever I can to your glory. Amen

REFLECTIVE QUESTIONS

1. What else could you do to make the most out of your life?
2. If today is the last day that you will live, what do you need to do or say?
3. What are the things that you do that are a waste of time?
4. What unfinished business do you need to do before you die?

CHAPTER

5

SPIRITUAL CARE PLAN

A spiritual care plan summarizes the care to be given to the terminally ill and their family. It is a set of spiritual actions that help to address the dying persons' symptoms, aims and measured outcomes. It is a guide used to evaluate the effectiveness of the spiritual care that is rendered. A spiritual care plan is a strategy to overcome spiritual battles waged within the soul of those facing the end of their life. The dying, spiritual care worker and caregiver must work together to fight the good fight. A Spiritual Care Plan is life map to inner peace and a closer relationship with others and the divine. It ultimately leads to inner healing and spiritual harmony with all things. The Spiritual Care Plan is especially helpful for the hospice clinician.

Every spiritual care plan will include the terminally ills Symptoms, Aims and Measurement that can be summarized in an acrostic called **S.A.M.**

S - Is for **Symptoms** or the primary concerns of the dying. Some of these symptoms or concerns are: family, feelings, focus, finances, faults, faith and finite being. Or the dying may manifest spiritual sicknesses like toxic guilt, sadness, meaninglessness, anger, despair, alienation and hopelessness. Whatever the spiritual symptom or sickness is it should be recognized and addressed by the dying and the spiritual care provider.

A- Is for **Aim** or the goal of the terminally ill. The aims must be patient specific. The aim is always patient or family driven. It is not the goal of the spiritual care provider. The aim is the realistic expectation of the patient. It's what they want or hope for. The spiritual care provider will render spiritual interventions to assist the patient to fulfill their aim.

M-is for **measuring** the outcome. Measuring the outcome of the aim will determine the effectiveness of the spiritual care plan. When one measures the outcome it could either be met, unmet or ongoing. If it is *met* this means the patient has accomplished their aims. If it is *unmet* it means the dying persons has either been unable to accomplish their aims or they have rejected them. Or it could be that another kind of spiritual intervention is needed. Finally, if the terminally ill person is still attempting to fulfill their aims then it could be considered *ongoing*. The spiritual care provider will continue to use their interventions until the aim is met.

The **S.A.M** methodology for developing Spiritual Care Plan for the terminally ill is a simple tool that will enable the chaplain, social worker, hospice clinician, bereavement counselor and others to assess the dying person's symptoms, develop their aims and measure their effectiveness. To get a better understanding about how the **S.A.M** method is implemented some general case studies and their Spiritual Care Plans are provided.

CASE ONE

A sixty-nine-year-old woman dying of stomach cancer shared that she had been estranged from her oldest daughter. For over twenty years she has not seen or heard from her. She has tried to contact her through her family members but the daughter refuses to talk to her. The mother is heartbroken and feels rejected. The mother dying wish is that she would be able to see her daughter before she dies. The mother feels lonely, angry, and sad.

SPIRITUAL CARE PLAN

Symptoms	Aim	Measurement
Dysfunctional family	Patient's aim is to make phone calls to reconcile with daughter.	Met Patient made phone calls to daughter and began reconciliation process
Alienation	Patient's aim is to love herself by daily making self-affirming statements	Unmet Patient hasn't begun to affirm herself

CASE TWO

A fifty-two-year-old man diagnosed with lung cancer reluctantly accepted hospice care. He has shared that he is extremely angry with God and feels that God has cheated him out of his life. He firmly believes that God should give him more time to be with his family. He is frustrated and has given up on praying and reading the bible. His most painful disappointment is that God has not answered his prayers

SPIRITUAL CARE PLAN

Symptoms	Aim	Measurement
The patient has a controlling faith in that he demands that God answer his prayer and fulfill his dreams.	Patient will express a console dative faith that embraces suffering and death.	Unmet Chaplain will use learning based on scripture to assist patient in developing his faith and purpose in life
Patient is overwhelmed with bitterness and anger.	Patient will discover the beliefs and thoughts that under gird his anger.	Unmet Chaplain will use life review to help patient discover the source of his anger and bitterness

Patient has not accepted his terminality.	Patient will share that he has accepted his impending death.	Unmet Patient has not accepted his impending death Chaplain will use logo therapy to help patient find meaning in his death

CASE THREE

A Seventy-one-year-old woman dying of renal failure shared her anxiety and fears about the welfare of her adult children. She feels that her family will fall apart after her death. She is the matriarch of her family and her six children have become overly dependent on her. Moreover, her adult children do not get along very well. She is afraid to tell them the status of her illness for fear that they might not be able to cope.

SPIRITUAL CARE PLAN

Symptoms	Aim	Measurement
Patient's fears impact her family relationship	Patient will share her faith and trust in Gods care for her family	ongoing Chaplain will use learning based on the bible to assist patient in developing trust and faith in God
Patient family is fragmented	Patient will meet with entire family to share their thoughts and feelings	Ongoing Patient has not met all of the family chaplain will use life review to help patient understand family history

CASE FOUR

A sixty-two-year-old man is dying of a brain tumor is frustrated and angry. He just retired and he recently found out about his illness. He sits at home miserable and bored letting the days go by. He feels there is nothing else to live for. He doesn't want to leave his home or have any visitors. He doesn't talk on the phone or socialize with his neighbors

SPIRITUAL CARE PLAN

Symptoms	Aim	Measurement
The patient has a lack of meaning in life	The patient will develop a new purpose for living	ongoing Patient is open to chaplain using logo therapy to assist patient in developing a new purpose in life
Patient is alienated from friends and family	Patient will participate in social activities	ongoing Patient has not participated in activities Chaplain will emphasize love, forgiveness and reconciliation

CASE FIVE

A thirty-three-year-old male dying of AIDS is feeling guilty because he no longer has a relationship with his immediate family. He has come to the point in his life that he wants a closer relationship with his family. Unfortunately, some of them do not feel the same way toward him.

SPIRITUAL CARE PLAN

Symptoms	Aim	Measurement
Patient has toxic guilt	The patient will forgive himself for his relationships	ongoing Patient has not forgiven himself chaplain will emphasize self-love and grace of God
Patient has dysfunctional family	The patient will meet with family to lead them to point of acceptance	ongoing Patient is attempting to meet family Chaplain will at as advocate and peacemaker encouraging family reconciliation

CASE SIX

A Christian woman who just turned seventy years old has reluctantly accepted hospice care. She reads her bible constantly and prays every day for a miracle healing in her life. She firmly believes that she can be healed of her disease and get off of the hospice care.

SPIRITUAL CARE PLAN

Symptoms	Aim	Measurement
The patient has a controlling faith that doesn't accept unanswered prayer	The patient's aim is to develop a consolidative faith and can still accept unanswered prayer	Unmet Patient dogmatically believes her prayers will be answered Chaplain will validate patients faith until she is open to different biblical perspectives
Patient hasn't accepted death	Patient will learn to accept death and express it as healing	Unmet Patient is in denial about dying. Chaplain will support patients feelings and use logo therapy to assist patient in getting a different perspective

CASE SEVEN

A terminally ill male is dying of liver cancer. He has a history of substance abuse and his alcoholism has alienated him from his family. He is living in a nursing home. It is alleged that patient friends bring him something to drink when they visit. He doesn't really think he has a drinking problem.

SPIRITUAL CARE PLAN

Symptoms	Aim	Measurement
Patient has fault that manifest itself in alcoholism	Patient aim is to admit his fault and come to grips with his disease	Ongoing Patient has begun to see he has a drinking problem but still doesn't want to see its consequences Chaplain will use life review to help patient to see his drinking problem in relation to his family
Patient faith in himself and in God is weak	Patient will discover his inner spiritual resources to cope with substance abuse	Ongoing Patient has begun to realize he has relationship with God. Chaplain will

		use logo therapy and biblical teaching to help patient develop inner spiritual resources and relationship with God

CASE EIGHT

A fifty-five-year-old physically challenged man is a resident of the nursing home and feels bored. He has shared the emptiness of his life and yearns to do something. Moreover, he feels disconnected from many of the aged nursing home residents.

SPIRITUAL CARE PLAN

Symptoms	Aim	Measurement
The patient has lost focus and purpose in his life	The patient will develop a meaningful life	Ongoing Patient is open to creating a new purpose in his life. Chaplain will use logo therapy to assist patient in finding meaning in life
The patient is alienated from other residents and lacks social harmony	The patient will discover activities, programs and events that he can do with nursing home residents to give him a sense of social harmony	Met Patient has begun to attend facility activities like bingo, church services, and group music therapy

CASE NINE

A dying patient expressed her frustration with the level of care at her nursing home. She complains about the food, noise, and lack of sensitivity expressed by some of the aides. She wants to leave the nursing home but she is unable to. Family members shared that she has always been a constant complainer.

SPIRITUAL CARE PLAN

Symptoms	Aim	Measurement
The patient is frustrated with her life	The patient will develop an inner serenity and be willing to speak positively about her life	Unmet Patient continues to complain and is always negative. Chaplain will validate feelings and use life review to help patient look at positives in life and Gods presence
The patient is not pleased with her quality of life	The patient will tell facility staff about quality of life issues	Met Chaplain helped Patient to express her complaints in a positive way to facility staff

CASE TEN

A patient has multiple sclerosis and is no longer able to function and care for herself. The patient was once a vibrant and energetic high school teacher and is now wheelchair bound and has expressed purposelessness. She questions credibility of God and detached herself from others. She has become depressed.

SPIRITUAL CARE PLAN

Symptoms	Aim	Measurement
The patient no longer has a focus in life	The patient will develop a new focus in life and will express it	Ongoing Patient has begun to look at the things that she could do. Chaplain will use logo therapy to assist patient in creating a new life
The patient expresses a conventional faith that is unable cope with	The patient will develop a faith perspective that embraces disappointment and difficulties	Ongoing Patient has begun to read her bible with a new perspective. Chaplain will use biblical learning to help patient develop her faith

CASE ELEVEN

A young hospice patient has expressed his fears of dying and the eternal unknown. Often times the patient is agitated and anxious and finds it difficult to go to sleep. He said he fears being alone at the time of death.

SPIRITUAL CARE PLAN

Symptoms	Aim	Measurement
Fear:: The patient is restless and afraid of loss of health, control, and life	The patient will learn to eliminate feelings of helplessness and anxiety and reinstate calmness and trust in self, others and the Divine	Met Unmet On Going

CASE TWELVE

A twenty-three-year-old patient is overwhelmed with sadness and despair. He feels like giving up on himself, others, and on God. He shares his loss of routine, role and dreams that might have come true. He feels lonely, victimized and unhappy.

SPIRITUAL CARE PLAN

Symptoms	Aim	Measurement
Sadness/Despair: The patient is sad about multiple losses	The patients aim will be to find satisfaction in making difficult choices	Ongoing

Patient has begun to develop a new purpose and perspective in life with the assistance of chaplain who uses logo therapy |

CASE THIRTEEN

Mr. Jones is dying of congested heart failure. His impending death has made him have doubts about his God and others. He has become cynical, negative and pessimistic. Patient Jones has loss faith and refused to attend church or be visited by clergy.

SPIRITUAL CARE PLAN

Symptoms	Aim	Measurement
Doubt/Despair: The patient expressed a crushed faith perspective that has serious doubts about God and others	The patient will develop a consolidative faith that will embrace suffering and death	**Ongoing** Patient is beginning to reexamine his faith as chaplain uses biblical teaching and logo therapy to assist him.

CHAPTER

6

SPIRITUAL HEALING

Spiritual healing occurs when the needs and passions of the soul are fulfilled. Spiritual healing differs from physical healing in that it addresses the emotional, relational, psychological and existential needs of the soul. The dying can become spiritually healed through a variety of ways. Praying to God, counseling, logo therapy, listening to music, receiving and giving love, participating in an activity, engaging in religious activity, doing a hobby, spending quality time with people who genuinely love them, a stroll in the park, telling their life story, looking at family pictures, learning something new, playing with a pet, doing something that is healthy and happy. All of these things and much more can begin the process of spiritual healing. There are as many ways to receive spiritual healing as there are souls. Every soul is different and may require different spiritual interventions for it to be made whole. However, there is one universal spiritual intervention that can fulfill the spiritual needs of the soul.

One of the major ways in which the soul gets healed is through the reading, hearing, believing and meditating on the Word of God. The terminally ill need medicine for their sick body and their souls. The Word of God or the Bible is spiritual medicine that can heal the soul.

Spiritual healing can occur from hearing, believing and meditating on the Holy Scriptures.

The Bible is one of the greatest spiritual resources that we have at our disposal. There is no other book like the Bible. The Bible is the supreme book, supernatural in origin, divine in authorship, human in penmanship, infallible in authority and therapeutic in its effects. It has been called a map to guide us, a lamp to show us, a mirror to reveal us, milk that nourishes us, honey that sweetens us, a hammer that breaks us, a sword that defends us, a fire that warms us, meat that nourishes us, and medicine that heals us. The Bible is more than just words on a page, it is medicine for the soul.

There is not a feeling, belief, thought or behavior that the terminally ill may have that the Bible does not speak to. If their soul cries out in anguish the Bible has a message of comfort. If their soul is troubled the Bible instructs them on peace. If their soul is confronting death the Bible educates them on eternal life. Whatever the soul's sickness or weaknesses are the Bible has a word that fosters spiritual healing.

As a hospice chaplain, I have observed the powerful therapeutic effects of the Word of God on those who were dying. Reading the Bible has inspired many who were at the end of their lives. One 85-year-old hospice patient with terminal restlessness kept crying out saying, "Help me, somebody help me." The nurse came to her room and offered her pain medication, but she declined it. She said she wasn't in physical pain. The social worker visited her and tried to console her. But the woman was inconsolable. She continued to cry out, "Help me, somebody help me." This woman was not in physical or emotional pain. She was experiencing spiritual pain or distress. I began to read the Bible to her and she began to settle down and calmness came over her. Miraculously she stopped shouting and moving her arms and legs aimlessly. The more I read the Bible to her the more peaceful she had become. As I read the 23rd Psalm, she began to smile and softly recited the words with me. She was at peace and her terminal restlessness came to an end. What happened in this situation? God, the Holy Physician healed her restless soul through His spiritual medicine, the Holy Bible. This woman needed more than pain medication she needed spiritual healing that came from hearing the Word of God.

All clergy, nurses, social workers, grief counselors, health aides and caregivers must be prepared to facilitate spiritual healing. Reading the Bible is one of the ways to give spiritual healing to the terminally ill. The following index of the soul's needs and spiritual healing found in the scripture has been compiled. The care provider can diagnose the souls need by listening to the feelings and thoughts of the dying. Then they can read the appropriate scripture which will foster spiritual healing. Or if it is physically possible the terminally ill can read and meditate on the Holy Scriptures for their own spiritual wellbeing.

THE SOULS NEED AND SPIRITUAL HEALING

1. When the soul needs companionship
2. When the soul needs comfort
3. When the soul needs hope
4. When the soul needs joy
5. When the soul needs courage
6. When the soul is struggling to accept death
7. When the soul is anxious and worried
8. When the soul needs peace
9. When the soul needs patience
10. When the soul seeks God
11. When the soul seeks healing
12. When the soul is guilty and needs forgiveness
13. When the soul is afraid
14. When the soul needs guidance
15. When the soul is angry and frustrated

16. When the soul needs to forgive others
17. When the soul seeks Gods will
18. When the soul is prayerful
19. When the soul needs more faith
20. When the soul is persevering
21. When the soul is seeking holiness
22. When the soul is frustrated
23. When the soul seeks eternal life

1. WHEN THE SOUL NEEDS COMPANIONSHIP

"I will not leave you without help as children without help as children without parents, I will come to you." John 14:18

"Then you will call, and the Lord will answer. You will cry, and He will say, "Here I am". Isaiah 58:9

"I will be a Father to you. You will be my sons and daughters, says the All-Powerful God." II. Corinthians 6:18

"See I am with you. I will care for you everywhere you go. And I will bring you again to this land. For I will not leave you until I have done all things I promised." Genesis 28:15

"Because I suffer and am in need, let the Lord think of me. You are my help and the One who sets me free. O my God, do not wait." Psalm 40:17

"The Lord is with you when you are with him. If you look for Him, he will let you find him. But if you leave him, He will leave you."

"You will look for me and find me, when you look for me with all your heart. I will be found by you." Jeremiah 29:13-14

"When you pass through the waters. I will be with you. When you pass through the rivers, they will not flow over you. When you walk through the fire, you will not be burned. The fire will not destroy you." Isaiah 43:2

2. WHEN THE SOUL NEEDS COMFORT

"God is our refuge and our strength. A very present help in time of trouble. Therefore, we will not fear. Thou the earth be removed. Thou the mountains quake with swelling thereof." Psalm 46:1-3

"The Lord is my Rock and my safe place and the one who takes me out of trouble. My God is my Rock, in whom Aim safe. He is my safe keeping, my saving strength and my strong tower." Psalm 18:2

"For he has not turned away from the suffering of the one in pain or trouble. He has not hidden His face from Him, but He has heard his cry for help." Psalm 22:24

"When he falls, he will not be thrown down, because the Lord holds his hand." Psalm 37:24

"Give all your strength to the Lord and He will give you strength. He will never let those who are right with Him be shaken." Psalm 55:22

"Come to me, all who labor and are heavy laden. I will give your rest." Matthew 11:28

3. WHEN THE SOUL NEEDS HOPE

"Why are you sad, O my soul? Why have you become troubled within me? Hope in God, for I will yet praise Him, my help and my God." Psalm 42:11

"Because of Christ, you have put your trust in God He raised Christ from the dead and gave Him great honor. So now your faith and hope are in God." I. Peter 1:21

"Christ in you the hope and glory." Colossians 1:27

"For you are my hope, O Lord God. You are my trust since I was young." Psalm 71:5

"Be strong in heart, all you who hope in the Lord." Psalm 31:24

"Let us thank the God and Father of our Lord Jesus Christ. It was through His loving-kindness that we were born again to a new life and have a hope that never dies. This hope is ours because Jesus was raised from the dead." I. Peter 1:3

"Hope never makes us ashamed because the love of God has come into our hearts through the Holy Spirit who has given to us." Romans 5:5

4. WHEN THE SOUL NEEDS JOY

"You have filled my heart with more happiness than they have when there is much grain-wine." Psalm 4:7

"You will show me the way of life. Being with you is to be full of joy." Psalm 16:11

"The joy of being saved is being heard in the tents of those who are right and good. The right hand of the Lord does powerful things." Psalm 118:15

"Yet I will have joy in the Lord. I will be glad in the God who saves me." Habakkuk 3:18

"For our heart is full of joy in Him, because we trust in His Holy name." Psalm 33:21

"Do not be sad for the joy of the Lord is your strength." Nehemiah 8:10

5. WHEN THE SOUL NEEDS COURAGE

"Wait on the Lord and be strong. Let your heart be strong. Yes, wait for the Lord." Psalm 27:14

"He gives strength to the weak. And He gives power to Him who has little strength." Isaiah 40:29

"Have I not told you? Be strong and have strength of heart? Do not be afraid or lose faith. For the Lord your God is with you anywhere you go." Joshua 1:9

"But now the Lord who made you, Jacob, and He who made you, O Israel, says, do not be afraid. For I bought and made you free. I have called you by name. You are mine! Isaiah 43:1

"Be strong. Be strong in heart, all you who hope in the Lord." Psalm 31:24

"The Lord is my Light and my salvation. Whom shall I fear? The Lord is the strength of my life, whom shall I be afraid." Psalm 27:1

6. WHEN THE SOUL IS STRUGGLING TO ACCEPT DEATH

"For sure, I tell you, if anyone keeps my word, that one will never die." John 8:51

"But God will free my soul from the power of the grave. For He will take me to Himself."

Psalm 49:15

"He will take away death for all time. The Lord God will dry tears from all faces." Isaiah 25:8

"Then whoever puts his trusts in Him will have everlasting life." John 3:15

"Yea thou I walk through the valley of the shadow of death. I will fear no evil. For thou art with me." Psalm 23:5

"He will take away death for all time. The Lord God will dry tears from all faces." Isaiah 25:8

"This is the reason we do not give up. Our human body is wearing out. But our spirits are getting stronger every day." II. Corinthians 4:16

"I am the Resurrection and the Life. He that believeth in me, though he may die, will not perish but have everlasting life. And whoever lives and believes in me shall never die." John 11:24-26

"I am the living Bread which came down from heaven. If anyone eats of this Bread, he will live forever and the bread that I shall give is my flesh, which I shall give for the life of the world." John 6:51

"Then they came to a place which was named Gethsemane and He said to His disciples, sit here while I pray. And He took Peter, James and John with Him, and He began to be troubled and deeply distressed. Then He said to them, my soul is exceedingly sorrowful, even to death. Stay here and watch. He went a little further and he fell on the ground and prayed that if it were possible the hour might pass from Him. And He said, Abba Father, all things are possible for you. Take this cup away from me; nevertheless, not my will by thy will be done." Mark 14:32-36

7. WHEN THE SOUL IS WORRIED

"Do not worry. Learn to pray about everything. Give thanks to God as you ask Him for what you need. The peace of God is much greater than human mind can understand. This peace will keep your hearts and minds through Christ Jesus." Philippians 4:6-7

"And my God will give everything according to His riches in Christ Jesus." Philemon 4; 1p

"Do not worry. Do not keep saying, what will we eat or what will we drink or what will we wear? The people who do not know God are looking for all these things. Your Father in Heaven knows you need all these things." Matthew 6:31-32

"Give all your worries to Him because He cares for you." I. Peter 5:7

8. WHEN THE SOUL NEEDS PEACE

"Let the peace of Christ have power over your hearts, you were chosen as a part of His body. Always be thankful." Colossians 3:15

"The peace of God is much greater than the human mind can understand. This peace will keep your hearts and minds through Christ Jesus." Philippians 4:7

"May the Lord give you peace. His peace at all times. The Lord be with you all." II. Thessalonians 3:16

"Peace I leave with you. My peace I give to you. I do not give peace to you as the world gives. Do not let your hearts be troubled or afraid." John 14:27

"Thou wilt keep him in perfect peace whose mind is stayed on thee." Isaiah 26:3

"Be anxious for nothing but in everything by prayer and supplication with thanksgiving let your request be made known to God and the peace of which surpasses all understanding will guard your hearts and minds through Christ Jesus." Philippians 4:6, 7

9. WHEN THE SOUL NEEDS PATIENCE

"Therefore, be patience brethren until the coming of the Lord. See how the farmer waits for the precious fruit of the earth until it receives the early and latter rain. You also be patient. Establish your hearts for the coming of the Lord is at hand. "James 5:7, 8

"And let us not grow weary in well doing for in due season you shall reap if you faint not." Galatians 6:9

"Let us hold fast the confession of our hope without wavering for He who promised is faithful." Hebrews 10:23

"My brethren count it all joy when you fall into various trials knowing that the testing of your faith produces patience. But let patience have its perfect work that you may be perfect and complete lacking nothing." James 1:2-4

10. WHEN THE SOUL SEEKS GOD

"The Lord is with you while you are with Him. If you seek Him, He will be found by you; but if you forsake Him, He will forsake you. "II. Chronicles 14:7

"But without faith it is impossible to please Him, for he who comes to God must believe that He is, and that He is a rewarder of those who diligently seek Him." Hebrew 11:6

"But from there you will seek the Lord your God, and you will find Him if you seek Him with all your heart and with all your soul." Deuteronomy 4:28

"And you will seek me and find me when you search for me with all your heart." Jeremiah 29:13

"The Lord is good to those who wait for Him, to the one who looks for Him." Lamentations 3:25

11. WHEN THE SOUL SEEKS HEALING

"Heal me, O Lord, and I will be healed. Save me and I will be saved. For you are my praise." Jeremiah 17:14

"Serve the Lord your God and He will give you bread and water. And I

take sickness from among you." Exodus 23:5

"For I will heal you. I will heal you where you have been hurt, says the Lord "Jeremiah 30:17

"He carried our sins in His own body when He died on a cross. In doing this, we may be dead to sin and alive to all that is right and good. His wounds have healed you." I. Peter 2:24

"But He was hurt for our wrong doing. He was crushed for our sins. He was punished so we would have peace. He was beaten so we would be healed." Isaiah 53:5

12. WHEN THE SOUL IS GUILTY AND NEEDS FORGIVENESS

"You know that Christ came to take away our sins. There is no sin in Him." I. John 3:5

"The next day John the Baptist saw Jesus coming to him. He said, "The Lamb of God who takes away the sin of the world." John 1:29

"Because of the blood of Christ, we are bought and made free from the punishment of sin. And because of His blood, our sins are forgiven. His loving favor to us is so rich." Ephesians 1:7

"He gave Himself to die for our sins. He did this so we could be saved from this sinful world." Galatians 1:4

"The Lord is merciful and gracious slow to anger, and abounding in mercy. He will not always strive with us. Nor will he keep His anger forever. He has not dealt with us according to our sins, nor punished us according to our iniquities. For as the heavens are high above the earth, So great is His mercy toward those who fear Him; As far as the east is from the west, So far has He removed our transgression from us. As a father pities his children so the Lord pities those that fear Him." Psalm 103:8-13

"If we confess our sins, He is faithful and just and will forgive our sins and cleanse us from all unrighteousness." I. John 1:9

"I will show loving kindness to them and forgive their sins. I will remember their sins no more." Hebrews 8:12

"I will make them clean from all the sins they have done against me. I will forgive all their sins against me." Jeremiah 33:8

"I, even I, am the One who takes away your sins because of who I am. And I will not remember your sins." Isaiah 43:25

13. WHEN THE SOUL IS FEARFUL

"Do not be afraid, little flock. Your Father wants to give you the kingdom." Luke 12:32

"For I am the Lord God who holds your right hand, and who says to you, do not be afraid. I will help you." Isaiah 41:13

"For God did not give us a spirit of fear. He gave us a spirit of power and of love and of a good mind." II. Timothy 1:7

"You will not be afraid when you lie down. When you lie down, your sleep will be sweet." Proverbs 3:24

"So we can say for sure, The Lord is my helper. I am not afraid of anything." Hebrews 13:6

"God is our safe place and our strength. He is always our help in time of trouble. So, we will not be afraid, even if the earth is shaken and the mountains fall into the center of the sea." Psalm 46:1-2

"Fear not, for you will not be ashamed. Do not be troubled, for you will not be put to shame." Isaiah 54:4

"Yea thou I walk through the valley of the shadow of death I will fear no evil. For thou art with me thy rod and thy staff comfort me." Psalm 23:4

"The Lord is my Light and my Salvation who shall I fear. The Lord is the strength of my life of whom shall I be afraid…Even if an army encamped against me, my heart will not fear. Even if war rises against me, I will be sure of you." Psalm 27:1, 3

14. WHEN THE SOUL IS LOST AND NEEDS GUIDANCE

"Your ears will hear a word behind you, saying this is the way walk in it, whenever you turn to the right or to the left." Isaiah 30:21

"This is God, our God forever and ever. He will show us the way until death." Psalm 48:14

"The steps of a good man are led by the Lord. And He is happy in his way." Psalm 37:23

"For his God tells him what to do and teaches him the right way."

"Trust in the Lord with all thine heart lean not to thy own understanding in all thy ways acknowledge Him and He shall direct thy paths." Proverbs 3:5-7

"I will lead the blind by the way that they do not know. I will lead them in the paths they do not know. I will turn darkness into light in front of them. And I will make the bad places smooth. These are the things I will do and I will not leave them." Isaiah 42:16

"Yet I am always with you. You hold me by my right hand. You will lead me by telling me what I should do. And after this, you will bring me into shining -greatness." Psalm 73:23-24

15. WHEN THE SOUL IS ANGRY

"My Christian brothers, you know that everyone should listen much and speak little. He should be slow to become angry. A man's anger does not allow him to be right with God." James 1:19-20

"Do not be quick in spirit to be angry. For anger is in the heart of fools." Ecclesiastes 7:9

"He who has a quick temper acts in a foolish way, and a man who makes sinful plans is hated." Proverbs 14:17

"A man of anger starts fights, and a man with a bad temper is full of a wrong-doing. "Proverbs 29:22

"Stop being angry. Turn away from fighting. Do not trouble yourself. It leads to wrong doing." Psalm 37:8

"A gentle answer turns away anger, but a sharp word causes anger." Proverbs 15:1

"If you are angry, do not let it become sin. Get over your angry before the day is finished." Ephesians 4:26

"A man's understanding makes him slow to anger. It is to his honor to forgive and forget a wrong done to him." Proverbs 19:11

"Put out of your life all these things: bad feelings about other people, anger, temper, and loud talk, bad talk which hurts other people, and bad feelings which hurt other people. You must be kind to each other. Think of the other person. Forgive other people just as God forgave you because of Christ's' death on the cross." Ephesians 4:31-32

"Christian brothers, never pay back someone for the bad he has done to you. Let the anger of God take care of the other person. The Hoy Writings say, I will pay back to them what they should get, says the

Lord. If the one who hate you is hungry feed him... If he is thirsty give him water. If you do that, you will be making him more ashamed of himself. Do not let sin have power over you. Let good have power over sin." Romans 12:19-21

16. WHEN THE SOUL NEEDS TO FORGIVE OTHERS

"When you stand to pray, if you have anything against anyone, forgive him. Then your Father in heaven will forgive your sins also." Mark 11:25

"If you forgive people their sins, your Father in heaven will forgive your sins also." Matthew 6:14

"But love those who have you. Do well to them. Let them use your things and do not expect something back. Your pay will be much. You will be children of the Most High. He is kind to those who are not thankful and to those who are full of sin. You must have loving-kindness just as your Father has loving-kindness. Do not say what is wrong in others people's lives. Then other people will not say what is wrong in your life. Do not say someone is guilty. Then other people will not say you are guilty. Forgive other people and other people will forgive you. Give, and it will be given to you. You will have more than enough. It can be pushed down and shaken together and it will run over as it is given to you. The way you give to others is the way you will receive in return." Luke 6:35-38

"Do not say, I will punish wrongdoing. Wait on the Lord, and He will take care of it." Proverbs 20:22

17. WHEN THE SOUL SEEKS GODS WILL

"Seek first His Kingdom and His Righteousness and all those things shall be added unto you." Matthew 6:33

"Trust in the Lord with all thine heart lean not to thine own understanding and He shall give thee the desires of thine heart." Proverbs 3:5-7

"I will lift up mine eyes unto the hills from whence comes my help. My help cometh from the Lord which made heaven and earth." Psalm 121:1, 2

"I will instruct you and teach you in the way you should go. I will guide you with my eye." Psalm 32:8

"However, when He, the Spirit of truth, has come, He will guide you into all truth; for He will not speak on His own authority, but whatever He hears He will speak; and He will tell you things to come." John 16:13

"The entrance of your words gives light; it gives understanding to the simple." Psalm 119:130

"Commit your works to the lord, and your thoughts will be established." Proverbs 16:3

"I will bring the blind by a way they did not know; I will lead them in paths they have not known. I will make darkness light before them, and crooked places straight. These things I will do for them, and not forsake them." Isaiah 42:16

"With Him are wisdom and strength, He has counsel and understanding." Job 12:13

"If any of you lacks wisdom, let him ask of God, who gives to all liberally and without reproach, and it will be given to Him." James 1:5

18. WHEN THE SOUL IS PRAYERFUL

"And whatever you ask in my name, that I will do, that the Father may be glorified in the Son. If you ask anything in my name, I will do it." John 14:13-14

"And all things, whatever you ask in prayer, believing, you will receive." Matthew 21:22

"If you abide in me, and my words abide in you, you will ask what you desire, and it shall be done for you." John 15:7

"And the prayer of faith will save the sick, and the Lord will raise him up. And if he has committed sins, he will be forgiven. Confess your trespasses to one another, and pray for one another, that you may be healed. The effective, fervent prayer of a righteous man avails much." James 5:15-16

"Now this the confidence that we have in Him, that if we ask anything according to His will, He hears us. And if we know He hears us, whatever we ask, we know that we have petitions that we have asked of Him. I. John 5: 14, 15

"He shall call upon me, and I will answer him, I will answer him; I will be with him in time of trouble; I will deliver him and honor him." Psalm 91:15

"It shall come to pass that before they call, I will answer; and while they are still speaking, I will hear." Isaiah 65:24

"Then you will call upon me and go and pray to me, and I will listen to you. "Jeremiah 29:12

"Ask, and it will be given to you; seek, and you will find: knock, and it will be opened to you. For everyone who asks receives, and he who seeks finds, and to him who knocks it will be opened. If you then, being evil, know how to give good gifts to your children, how much more will your Father who is in heaven give good things to those who ask Him." Matthew 7:7-8, 11

"The Lord is near to all who call upon Him, to all who call upon Him in truth." Psalm 145:18

"He shall pray to God, and He will delight in him, He shall see His face with joy, for he restores to man his righteousness." Job 33:26

"Call to me, and I will answer you and show you great and mighty things which you do not know." Jeremiah 33:3

"Our Father who art in Heaven. Holy is thy name. Thy kingdom come. Thy will be done. On earth as it is in Heaven. Give us this day our daily bread. And forgive us our trespasses as we forgive those who trespass against us. And lead us not into temptation. But deliver us from evil. For thine is the kingdom and the power and the glory forever and ever. Matthew 6

"God grant me the serenity to accept the things that I can. The courage to change the things that I can. And the wisdom to know the difference." Serenity Prayer Reinhold Niebuhr

19. WHEN THE SOUL NEEDS MORE FAITH

"Now faith is the substance of things hope for, the evidence of things not seen." Hebrews 11:1

"But without faith it is impossible to please Him, for he who comes to God must believe that He is a rewarder of those who diligently seek Him." Hebrews 11:6

"And all these, having obtained a good testimony through faith, did not receive the promise, God having provided something better for us, that they should not be made perfect apart from us." Hebrews 11:39, 40

"For we walk by faith not by sight." II. Corinthians 5:7

20. WHEN THE SOUL IS PERSERVERING

"Whatever is born of God overcomes the world. And this is the victory that has overcome the world. And this is the victory that has overcome the world our faith. Who is he who overcomes the world, but he who believes that Jesus is the Son of God? I. John 5:4-5

"Therefore, do not cast away your confidence, which has a great reward. For you have need of endurance, so that after you have done the will of God, you may receive the promise." Hebrews 10:35-36

"He who overcomes shall be clothed in white garments, and I will not blot out his name from the Book of Life; but I will confess his name before My Father and before His angels." Revelations 3:5

"Let us hold fast the confession of our hope without wavering, for He who promised is faithful. And let us consider one another to stir up love and good works." Hebrews 10:23, 24

"Therefore, submit devil to God. Resist the devil and he will flee from you." James 4:7

"Then the Lord knows how to deliver the godly out of temptations and to reserve the unjust under punishment for the Day of Judgment." II. Peter 2:9

"He gives power to the weak, and to those who have no might He increases strength. Even the youths shall faint and be weary, and the young men shall utterly fall, but those who wait on the Lord shall renew their strength; they shall mount up with wings like eagles, they shall run and not be weary, they shall walk and not faint." Isaiah 40:29-31

"Be of good courage, and He shall strengthen your heart, all you who hope in the Lord."

Psalm 31:24

"So, I will strengthen them in the Lord and they shall walk up and down in His name, says the Lord." Zechariah 10:12

21. WHEN THE SOUL IS SEEKING HOLINESS

"Blessed are the pure in heart, for they shall see God." Matthew 5:8

"To the pure all things are pure, but to those who are defiled and unbelieving nothing is pure; but even their mind and conscience are defiled." Titus 1: 15

"Who may ascend into the hill of the Lord? Or who may stand in His Holy place? He who has clean hands and a pure heart, who has not lifted up his soul to an idol, nor sworn deceitfully." Psalm 24:3-4

"But you were washed, but you were sanctified, but you were justified in the name of the Lord Jesus and by the Spirit of our God." I. Corinthians 6:11

"And you, who once were alienated and enemies in your mind by wicked works, yet now He has reconciled in the body of His flesh through death, to present you holy, and blameless, and irreproachable in His sight." Colossians 1:21-22

"Now may the God of peace Himself sanctify you completely; and may your whole spirit, soul, and body be preserved blameless at the coming of our Lord Jesus Christ." I. Thessalonians 5:23

"Then I will give them one heart, and I will put a new spirit within them, and take the stony heart out of their flesh, and give them a heart of flesh, that they may walk in my statutes and keep my judgments and do them ; and they shall be my people, and I will be their God." Ezekiel 11:19-20

"But of Him you are in Christ Jesus, who became for us wisdom from God and righteousness and sanctification and redemption." I. Corinthians 1:30

22. WHEN THE SOUL IS FRUSTRATED

"You will keep him in perfect peace, whose mind is stayed on you, because he trusts in you." Isaiah 26:3

"Commit your way to the Lord, trust also in Him, and He shall bring it to pass." Psalm 37:5

"Beloved do not think it strange concerning the fiery trial which is to try you, as though some strange thing happened to you, but rejoice to the extent that you partake of Christ's sufferings that when His glory is revealed, you may be glad with exceeding joy." I. Peter 4:12-13

"Trust in the Lord with all your heart, and lean not on your own understanding; in all your ways acknowledge Him, and He shall direct your paths." Proverbs 3:5-6

"Great peace have those who love your law, and nothing causes them to stumble." Psalm 119:165

"When you pass through the waters, I will be with you; and through the rivers, they shall not overflow you. When you walk through the fire, you shall not be burned, nor shall the flame scorch you." Isaiah 43:2

"Cast your burden on the Lord, and He shall sustain you; He shall never permit the righteous to be moved." Psalm 55:22

"Be anxious for nothing, but in everything by prayer and supplication, with thanksgiving, let your request be made known to God; and the peace of God, which surpasses all understanding, will guard your hearts and minds through Christ Jesus." Philippians 4:6-7

"Rest in the Lord, and wait patiently for Him; do not fret because of him who prospers in his way, because of the man who brings wicked schemes to pass." Psalm 37:7

"Now this is the confidence that we have in him, that if we ask anything according to His will, he hears us. And if we know that he hears us, whatever we ask, we know that we have petitions that we have asked of Him." I. John 5:14-15

"He who did not spare His own Son, but delivered Him up for us all, how shall He not with Him also freely give us all things? Romans 8:32

23. WHEN THE SOUL SEEKS ETERNAL LIFE

"I am the living bread which came down from heaven, if anyone eats of this bread, he will live forever; and the bread that I shall give is my flesh, which I shall give for the life of the world. Whoever eats my flesh and drinks my blood has eternal life, and I will raise him up at the last day." John 6:51, 54

"God so loved the world that he gave his only begotten son so that whoever believeth in me should not perish but have everlasting life." John 3:16

"And this is the testimony: that God has given us eternal life, and this is in His Son. These things I have written to you who believe in the name of the Son of God, that you may know that you have eternal life, and that you may continue to believe in the name of the Son of God." I. John 5:11, 13

"Most assuredly, I say to you, he who hears my word and believes in Him who sent me has everlasting life, and shall not come into judgment, but has passed from death into life." John 4:14

"If you confess with your mouth the Lord Jesus and believe in your heart that God raised him from the dead you shall be saved."

Jesus said to her, "I am the resurrection and the life. He who believes in me, though he may die, he shall live. And whoever lives and believes in me, though he may die, he shall live. And whoever lives and believes in me shall never die. Do you believe this? "John 11:25-26

"For the wages of sin is death, but the gift of God is eternal life in Christ Jesus our Lord." Romans 6:23

BIBLIOGRAPHY

Atchley, A., *Spirituality and Aging*, Baltimore, John Hopkins, University Press.

Anderson, Herbert., *All Our Losses*, All Our Griefs. Westminster's Press., Philadelphia, 1983. worth

Boulden, Jim., *Life and Death*, Jim Boulden Publishers, CA., 1991.

Feifel, Herman., *The Meaning of Death.*, McGraw Hill Publishers, Toronto, 1965.

Koenig, H., *Aging and God: Spiritual Pathways to Mental Health in Midlife and Later Years*, New York: The Haworth Pastoral Press

Lord, Janice., *No Time For Goodbyes*, Pathfinder Publishers, CA., 1995.

Nouwen, Henri., Our Greatest Gift. San Francisco, Harper Collins,1985.

Ross, Elizabeth., On Death and Dying, MacMillian, New York., 1969.

Soulen, Richard., *Care for the Dying*, John Knox, Atlanta, 1978.

Staudacher, Carol., *Beyond Grief*, New Harbinger, CA., 1987.

About the Author

Dr. Samuel White III graduated with honors from Brockport State College with a Bachelor of Science. He went on to graduate from Harvard Divinity School with a Master of Theology degree and a Master of Divinity degree at the Methodist Theological School in Ohio. He completed his educational pursuit by achieving a Doctor of Ministry degree at Drew University. Dr. White's educational qualifications are complemented by his experiences as a pastor and a hospice chaplain. Dr. White currently serves as the pastor of the historic Friendship Baptist Church. It is under his leadership that Friendship Baptist Church has become a hospital for sin-sick souls providing spiritual healing. Dr. White has served as a chaplain for Hospices of Michigan and Hospices of Henry Ford conducting spiritual assessments and spiritual care for terminally ill patients and their grieving families. Since 1996, Dr. White has been married to the former Sandra Cannon. They are richly blessed with two children, Alexandria and Samuel IV.